Praise for *Subtle Acts of Exclusion*

"This is an unreasonable manifesto. It's unreasonable because it challenges us to take responsibility, to be kind, to dig in, and to change the invisible corners of our culture. We've got work to do. Unreasonable is precisely what we need."
—**Seth Godin, author of** *This Is Marketing*

"In my work, I have seen how Black people, especially young Black women, are frequently excluded by 'well-intentioned' people. Some of the exclusions are not subtle at all, but many of them are. The subtle ones are especially insidious and pervasive and hard to fight back against. This book skillfully uses stories and research to build a deep understanding that may actually be able to take something negative and turn it into an opportunity to productively come together and create more support, trust, and equity. Now that's a feat! Jana and Baran have found a way to give shape and depth to a topic that is difficult to grasp and difficult to speak up about because of its subtlety. But more than that, they have provided a language that we can all use to actually have open and productive conversations about topics that have become incredibly divisive. I can see applications of this framework not just for work but for higher education and beyond."
—**Aimee Meredith Cox, PhD, Director of Undergraduate Studies, Department of African American Studies, and Associate Professor, Departments of Anthropology and African American Studies, Yale University, and author of** *Shapeshifters*

"Tiffany Jana and Michael Baran have provided us a powerful tool to help us learn about how subtle forms of bias can profoundly impact people's sense of belonging and their ability to perform at the highest level. Through thoughtful research and powerful examples, they have not only brilliantly articulated the problem but also offered us a pathway to a solution. Kudos!"
—**Howard Ross, author of** *ReInventing Diversity*, *Everyday Bias*, **and** *Our Search for Belonging*

"This book should open the floodgates for people to tell their own stories of being subtly excluded at work, with a new language that will make it so much easier to address out in the open and create teachable moments. As a little person, I have experienced so many subtle acts of exclusion over my career, whether it's people telling me I look 'cute' or having to constantly fight for respect and validity. I wish every one of my colleagues over the years had been able to read this book!"
—**Becky Curran Kekula, Director, Disability Equality Index, Disability:IN**

SUBTLE
ACTS OF
EXCLUSION

SUBTLE ACTS OF EXCLUSION

How to Understand, Identify, and Stop Microaggressions

TIFFANY JANA

Author of *Overcoming Bias* and *Erasing Institutional Bias*

MICHAEL BARAN

Berrett–Koehler Publishers, Inc.

Berrett-Koehler Publishers, Inc.
1333 Broadway, Suite 1000
Oakland, CA 94612-1921
Tel: (510) 817-2277
Fax: (510) 817-2278
www.bkconnection.com

ORDERING INFORMATION
Quantity sales. Special discounts are available on quantity purchases by corporations,
associations, and others. For details, contact the "Special Sales Department" at the Berrett-
Koehler address above.
Individual sales. Berrett-Koehler publications are available through most bookstores. They
can also be ordered directly from Berrett-Koehler: Tel: (800) 929-2929; Fax: (802) 864-7626;
www.bkconnection.com.
Orders for college textbook/course adoption use. Please contact Berrett-Koehler: Tel:
(800) 929-2929; Fax: (802) 864-7626.

Distributed to the U.S. trade and internationally by Penguin Random House Publisher
Services.

Berrett-Koehler and the BK logo are registered trademarks of Berrett-Koehler Publishers, Inc.

Printed in the United States of America

Berrett-Koehler books are printed on long-lasting acid-free paper. When it is available, we
choose paper that has been manufactured by environmentally responsible processes. These
may include using trees grown in sustainable forests, incorporating recycled paper, minimizing chlorine in bleaching, or recycling the energy produced at the paper mill.

Library of Congress Cataloging-in-Publication Data
Names: Jana, Tiffany, author.
Title: Subtle acts of exclusion : how to understand, identify, and stop
   microaggressions / Tiffany Jana and Michael Baran.
Description: First edition. | Oakland, CA : Berrett-Koehler Publishers,
   [2020] | Includes bibliographical references and index.
Identifiers: LCCN 2019037410 | ISBN 9781523087051 (paperback) | ISBN
   9781523087075 (epub) | ISBN 9781523087068 (pdf)
Subjects: LCSH: Microaggressions. | Prejudices. | Social isolation. |
   Diversity in the workplace.
Classification: LCC BF575.P9 J354 2020 | DDC 155.8/2—dc23
LC record available at https://lccn.loc.gov/2019037410

First Edition
27 26 25 24 23 22 21 20   10 9 8 7 6 5 4 3 2

Book producer and text designer: Happenstance Type-O-Rama
Cover designer: Dan Tesser, Studio Carnelian

*I dedicate this book to my
incomparable daughter, Saba*

—TIFFANY JANA

✦

*For my love Jill and our inspiring children,
Rio, Solomon, Raphael, and Carmelo*

—MICHAEL BARAN

CONTENTS

INTRODUCTION
Changing Minds and Behavior

THIS IS A BOOK about the subtle, confusing, insidious things that people say and do that end up excluding people with marginalized identities. This happens even though, for the most part, people are not intending to exclude others at all. In fact, it's quite the opposite. They may be trying to compliment someone or learn more about a person or be funny or build closeness. For decades now, people have called these slights "microaggressions," but in this book we will use the term "subtle acts of exclusion" (SAE) as a way to better describe and communicate this phenomenon. If we are going to create spaces that are more inclusive, respectful, and collaborative, we must understand and address these interactions.

Most people believe they are well intentioned, good people who don't go around causing harm. When we do inadvertently cause harm, we are often confused or surprised at other people's responses. We may deem them overly sensitive and rely on our good intentions as cover for the impact of our actions. Unfortunately, our mindset and our behaviors are not always aligned. The authors of this book believe that to truly address subtle acts of exclusion, we need to collectively shift both our mindset and our behaviors.

This is the case because we tend to judge ourselves and others differently. We think to ourselves, "I had good intentions," or "I'm not prejudiced," while at the same time believing that others might be uncaring, selfish, or even intentionally mean when they violate our boundaries. We may wonder why our offenders didn't realize that they were putting us down. In this way, we may set the relational bar low for ourselves and high for others. "My good intentions are enough," we think to ourselves as we minimize our offenses against others. But when someone offends us, their good intentions are an insufficient excuse for their behavior. As coauthors, we believe that the bar should be equalized. We cannot accept simple excuses for ourselves and impose more substantial expectations on others. We need to set a higher bar for ourselves as well. The offenses described in this book are real, though the names and details have been changed. We write this to help both the offender and the offended. We all need support so we can move forward in kindness.

We write this book with the belief that a better way of relating across differences is really possible. In fact, we both have dedicated our adult lives and professions to that precise end. We, and countless others, long for a world where cross-cultural competency is the norm—where differences are celebrated and respected, and people are seen and acknowledged for the unique and individual essence they embody. We find ourselves quite far from that place now. But we offer this collection of experiences, perspectives, and tools so that you might help cocreate a new reality in which everyone is empowered to express who they are without fear of being put down or left out. This vision of a new, inclusive reality begins with a shift in the mind and ends with the embrace of new behaviors.

We begin our journey with an illustrative story that coauthor Baran witnessed firsthand.

> I was at a community conversation on race in Frederick, Maryland, near where I live. It was organized by the Frederick County Human Relations Commission. A rich diversity of people showed up on this particular evening to discuss how to talk with one

another about race issues. Normally, I'm the one facilitating or leading these types of conversations, so it was a nice change of pace to be a participant. The facilitator showed a video that encouraged people to speak up when someone says something offensive, even if they don't know exactly what to say. The discussion was positive and productive.

And then Elaine stood up to speak. Elaine is a white woman who dedicates much of her free time to working toward racial justice. So it was somewhat of a shock when she addressed Bryan, the African American man who had spoken before her, and said, "You were so articulate in the way you said that." Before she could even finish her comment, the room clamored for her to stop. She didn't realize what was happening and kept talking for a bit. She eventually stopped and asked, "What's going on?" At that point, someone in the audience said, "You just called that man 'articulate,' which is a microaggression, and we are stopping you."

Elaine protested, "But I was just trying to give him credit and compliment him. He said that really well. I wasn't being aggressive at all. What's the problem?" At this point, people tried to explain that a lot of it has to do with the word "articulate" and its history. They also explained that the word communicated that Elaine was surprised that Bryan was so well spoken. I'm not sure if it ever became clear to her amid the confusion. I think Elaine was mortified because she was trying to do everything right—to compliment and give credit where credit was due.

In a nutshell, that's what's confusing about subtle acts of exclusion—they happen when people are not intending to do anything bad. In fact, they even happen when people are trying hard to be their best selves at a community conversation specifically on race! Good people commit SAE. Actually, everyone does, including the authors of this book. They do so because of a lack of understanding about other people's experiences or they do so because of unconscious biases. They do it at home, they do it in public spaces, and they do it at work. But because of the subtlety and confusion surrounding SAE, people often find it hard to speak up when it happens. Instead of having a productive conversation, we end up with silence, resentment, ignorance, and tension. We wrote this book to improve this situation by building a common understanding and language around SAE and a common framework for what to do when subtle acts of exclusion happen.

We have found that many people in our own corporate and community workshops and keynotes react similarly to Elaine, surprised to hear that calling someone "articulate" would be considered a microaggression, or SAE. They might ask in disbelief, "So I'm not allowed to compliment someone?" We have experienced firsthand people's confusion over microaggressions, thinking that what matters is the speaker's intent, when in fact what matters is the impact of the acts. We have witnessed people getting exasperated, thinking that you can't say anything anymore without someone getting upset. However, we want to reassure you that's not the case. In fact, it's easy to learn how to compliment someone without committing a subtle act of exclusion in the process. If the woman in the community conversation had said, "Great point, Bryan!" no one would have thought twice about it.

This book aims to build a new kind of deep understanding around subtle acts of exclusion that will help all of us commit fewer of them in the future. As authors, our goal is to help readers move beyond a vague feeling that something isn't right when they overhear or experience an SAE. We want readers to have a better understanding of why it isn't right and be able to articulate the reasons.

And the book recognizes that SAE are not going to disappear tomorrow. As such, we provide guidelines for what to do when these exclusions happen at work and beyond. We want people to feel comfortable and confident speaking up to address SAE when they see or hear them. This book clarifies that it is everyone's responsibility to speak up, and it helps readers know what to say when they do speak up. We give people a clear set of guidelines on how to speak up if an SAE is experienced, if it is just overheard, or if you are the person that committed the SAE. We also address what organizations can do to support these individual efforts and to facilitate moving their cultures toward more inclusivity.

The deep understanding we build and the guidelines for practical action come from our unique collaboration as authors who have different identities, privileges, and educational experiences but who have arrived at a similar professional place with a common vision. To that end, we offer a little bit about who we are and why this work matters to us.

DR. TIFFANY JANA:

> When you walk through life at the intersections, the halfway points between two truths or two polarities, it affects you. I am "intersectional" in the original sense of the term, coined by Dr. Kimberlé Crenshaw, in that I have lived most of my life identifying as female and Black. The world still experiences me mostly as female, but my gender identity has evolved to a new intersection. Again I am in the middle of multiple truths. And it's less my identity that has evolved as my understanding of who I am and the language I have access to.
>
> This book means so much to me personally because I get to leverage my professional experience as a global diversity, equity, and inclusion consultant in service of greater connection between humans. I spend my life helping individuals, communities, and leaders increase their cultural fluency, their empathy for people different from them. My goal is to help humankind cultivate a sense of belonging and genuine inclusion for all people.
>
> I come to this, my fourth book, as a Black, a gender nonbinary, a Christian, an invisibly disabled, a domestic violence survivor, and an LGBTQIA person who grew up speaking Spanish and German and traveling the world. I've been on welfare and I have enjoyed the privileges of professional success. I'm a mother, a divorcee, an artist, and an academic. All of these identities have

profoundly informed my experiences and shaped the way I think, act, and live.

While I have certainly experienced my fair share of microaggressions—as well as initiated far too many to enumerate—my identities have done exponentially more than make me a target or a victim. In fact, my multiple identities, including being Black identified with multiracial DNA from all over the globe, have fueled my empathy for more of humanity than most people. You see, it's easy to empathize with people who are like you. When you see yourself reflected in another person's experiences or situation, your heart extends toward them and sometimes you feel their joy and their pain almost as if it were your own. The same is not intrinsically true for people with whom you don't have as much in common.

When race, nationality, sexual orientation, gender, faith, political affiliation, socioeconomic class, disability, and other identities differ greatly from our own, we can sometimes dismiss the pain and experiences of others far too quickly. Of course, this is not universally true. But if it were not true, we would not need movements like #BLM (Black Lives Matter—against violence and systemic racism toward Black people), #MeToo (against sexual harassment and sexual assault), and #WontBeErased (civil rights for transgender people) to raise the voice and visibility of those suffering the injustice of a societal lack of compassion. My connectedness to so many communities, particularly the more historically marginalized ones, affords me the privilege of seeing, feeling, and understanding a broad array of experiences. When someone else's pain becomes your own, it's easier to serve your fellow human as an ally and a coconspirator instead of just a paralyzed bystander.

I have multiple advanced business degrees, have founded three diversity-focused companies, and have two decades of experience as an inclusion advocate and practitioner. This is why so much of what I offer in this book is framed through an organizational lens. I do believe that our institutions can be wonderful places to organically come together across differences and hone some of these deeply urgent interpersonal skills. The skills and tools presented in this book will not only help create stronger, more resilient organizational cultures, but they will also help create tighter bonds, increase empathy, and nurture a sense of psychological safety and belonging.

Though there is a strong organizational focus, the content has utility for any person interested in or ready to do the work of being a better, more informed, and compassionate person. I believe strongly that true freedom lies in the ability to embrace who you are without fear—to shine your light and be seen and appreciated—without the exhaustion of having to justify your very existence. I do pray that my experiences, identities, and perspectives help you on your journey to becoming a more intentionally inclusive ally who cultivates a sense of belonging for all people.

DR. MICHAEL BARAN:

Unlike Tiffany, I walk through the world with a lot of privilege, making it so I am not the subject of many subtle acts of exclusion. By "privilege," I don't mean that I am rich or that I grew up having everything handed to me. I mean that my gender, sexuality, and race don't make it harder for me in my daily life, and in fact confer both overt and hidden advantages. As a heterosexual white man, married with kids, it's rare that I ever even experience subtle acts of exclusion. As a Jewish person, I experience SAE around religion sometimes, though that's only a small part of what led me to the perspectives in this book.

I grew up in a fairly homogenous small town in Connecticut. As a young adult, I certainly hadn't heard about diversity and inclusion work, but was unknowingly launched into that career trajectory by the relationships I formed as I got to know a more diverse group of people. I learned from people who, unlike me, did feel marginalized, did face injustices and inequalities, and did experience subtle acts of exclusion. It felt so clearly wrong, unfair, and seemingly avoidable. I had many questions about why it was historically so common for humans to exploit others, form unequal societies, and discriminate against groups of people both consciously and unconsciously.

I turned to those questions in graduate school. To me and my colleagues and mentors in cultural anthropology and cognitive psychology at the University of Michigan, it seemed that answering those questions required a deep understanding of both culture and cognition—how human thinking works based on cultural input and experiences. The eight years I spent investigating those questions played a truly formative role in the way I came to see the world, the way I approach my diversity and inclusion work, and the way I think about topics such as the ones in this book.

But studying brains and culture can be tricky, for different reasons. Studying one's own culture is sometimes challenging because we take so many things for granted and don't even notice. I don't know who said it first, but you can think of culture for humans like water to a fish. It's everywhere and therefore hard to even see or contemplate. So one of the things anthropologists often do is go somewhere unfamiliar to do their research for an extended period to gain a more objective perspective on culture itself. In the beginning, so much is unfamiliar and you have to ask about everything, the explicit and the implicit. And eventually, through everyday living in that culture and through extensive systematic research, you get pretty good at picking out subtle cultural messages and underlying patterns of thinking. That is helpful as you analyze your research and also as you go about any new projects in your "home" culture.

In terms of brains, psychologists had been trying to study how the mind works from laboratory experiments with mostly undergraduate students who agreed to participate in research studies for credit when they took introductory psychology classes. But doing research in a controlled lab context with just college undergraduates is a limited way to figure out how human minds work more generally. Many psychologists have come to see that the research must be conducted with a wider sample of the human population and that the experiments must be conducted in a more real-world context.

Because of those challenges, I decided to do my fieldwork in Northeast Brazil for two years using a combination of qualitative participant observation (deep immersion into everyday life) and quantitative experiments that were more based in real-world contexts and scenarios. I wanted to try to answer for myself some critical questions that social scientists were debating. Is "race" in Brazil really different than it is in the United States or is it fundamentally the same? How are the ways that Brazilians think about race learned from cultural messages? And how do the cognitive categories of race influence how discrimination plays out in Brazil? The idea is that by answering those questions in a specific place, you learn something about how identity and discrimination work more broadly and can apply that understanding anywhere in the world.

To study those complex questions, I decided to do my investigations with children of different ages—to see how the learning happens from the youngest ages up through adulthood. And it just happened to be a fascinating time to study this in Belmonte in the Brazilian state of Bahia, when the cultural messages were going through a big transition. One year children were taught in schools that everyone was *morena*, or "brown" and racially mixed. The next year, children were taught that there was no such thing as brown and that everyone was either Black or white.

The experience of living there and focusing my attention on these research questions informs my approach to diversity and inclusion work in several ways. First, I learned to really listen to people and their experiences of exclusion, which sometimes broke down along lines I wouldn't have first expected. I couldn't rely on my preconceptions. That training helps me keep listening with close attention and empathy to people today, whether in the United States or around the world. During the writing of this book, for example, I interviewed more than a hundred people about the subtle exclusions they experience at work. Those interviews were instructive to us—helping make sure our examples were based on a wide diversity of real people and lived experiences. But those experiences can also be instructive to you. Many of those interviews were recorded on video, and clips from those interviews have been used for a digital program that can deepen the learning around SAE after you have read this book. (Go to *www.subtleactsofexclusion.com* to find out more about this digital program, including bringing it to your organization.)

Second, I learned to recognize how cultures can be infused with subtle messages about what is normal or not normal, good or bad. Those messages get reinforced through representations we can see and hear but also through daily interactions like subtle acts of exclusion. Seeing how that happens is essential if our goal is to eventually help people see how to interrupt those problematic interactions and create different and more inclusive messages about everyone being normal and good. That was one of my main inspirations for writing this book—to share what I learned about the subtlety and complexity of culture with you (without your having to take eight years to become a cultural anthropologist!).

Third, I learned to appreciate people's strong worldviews and the way they tend to dig in their heels when faced with information that contradicts their beliefs. People like to think they are good people with good intentions and can have strong defensive reactions when someone points out an SAE that they inadvertently committed. As such, I started working on ways to open people up to those conversations, to inoculate against the defensiveness when building deep understanding. I then refined and honed some of those strategies from years of working in the field of strategic frame communications for social issues. The strategies don't always work perfectly, but they can be highly effective for reaching people who may be skeptical or resistant.

Overall, I approach this work with that combination of practicality, curiosity, and passion. Having seen how cultures and brains work to create systems and patterns of thinking that result in injustices, I can also see how we can undo those patterns and create more equity and inclusion for all, both in the short term and in the future. I hope to use my privilege and perspective to reach wide audiences and create lasting cultural change. Tiffany and I hope our collaboration and complementary perspectives can make a significant contribution to that path forward.

We want this book to be useful for everyone. If you are sick of people asking where you are from because you look "exotic," this book is for you. If you are in HR at a company where SAE are happening and you don't know what to do about them, this book is for you. If you are a teacher or administrator in education and are concerned about SAE happening among students or coming from teachers, this book is for you. If you have never really thought much about any of this, this book is also for you.

This book is a resource for allies of all races, genders, religions, sexualities, abilities, and other demographics as you search for ways to increase your cultural fluency and advocacy—your understanding of what others experience and your ability to stand up as an ally in everyday interactions. The majority of people want to be better and more inclusive but can't find resources to help them do that. You may be wondering whether this is a book written only for white people. The answer is no. First, as we mentioned, everyone commits subtle acts of exclusion sometimes, even people with marginalized identities. And second, we also expect the book to provide insight and strategies for those who experience SAE all the time and are looking for useful tools to interrupt the problematic behavior.

If each of us spoke up every time we saw or heard an SAE taking place, we would get better at those conversations, and we'd have a lot more understanding and empathy. We wouldn't be so worried that committing an SAE makes us a "racist" or a bad person. We'd recognize that we all mess up sometimes, and the only thing that would really be a problem is if we didn't try to improve our behavior after we got that feedback. We'd have less tension around sensitive issues and more civility and transparency. And by civility, we don't mean excessive superficial politeness, but rather engaging, thoughtful conversations in which people work together to address an SAE that happened.

Speaking up is hard, knowing what to say is hard, receiving critical feedback is hard too. None of these is as hard as constantly getting excluded by SAE and having people neglect or deny that it is going on. We all have the strength to address this together and to build stronger, more diverse communities of trust. Having these conversations will build that trust, for stronger workplaces and for healthier, happier people and communities.

1

There's Nothing Micro about It

THE TERM "MICROAGGRESSION" originated in the early 1970s
with the work of Harvard psychiatrist Chester M. Pierce.[1] First
applied to describe insults against Black Americans and later against
women, it has now become largely accepted as a way for people to
talk about a wide range of issues related to discrimination, offense,
and exclusion against any marginalized group. The term itself is
well known in certain circles but largely unknown to most people.
It's most used in the context of higher education, linked to a growing consciousness of students who speak up for injustices they see,
including subtle verbal injustices in the classroom and on campus.

The Reaction against the Concept of Microaggressions and Our Response

In recent years, there have been varied strong negative reactions
against the term microaggression and a related term, "trigger warning."[2] Here we describe four common arguments.

First, people sometimes think that this is political correctness run amok. They may think that people are being policed for the small things they say, and therefore it is impossible to speak about any challenging issues. You can see this kind of reaction very strongly among conservatives, but even among many liberals and progressives, who think that sensitivity to the subtleties of language really is taking the concept of microaggression and injustice too far. One popular *New York Magazine* article by Jonathan Chait from a few years ago, for example, claimed that microaggressions were part of a larger politically correct stance "that people should be expected to treat even faintly unpleasant ideas or behaviors as full-scale offenses."[3]

The key idea here is that these critics are taking the "micro" part of "microaggressions" to heart, arguing that they are not a big deal compared to the more serious kinds of racism and other -isms that we recognize as problems. Explicit segregation and inequality were a big deal and are worth fighting against. But we've come a long way and made progress on those sorts of things. Paying attention to these seemingly little and subtle slights is just distracting and almost insulting to the real racism that existed. At least that's how the story goes.

Second, people may argue that even if the microaggression causes harm, it is everyone's right under free speech to say it anyway. They imagine that people fighting for social justice are literally telling people that they cannot say certain things, which they consider an assault on free speech. Groups such as Speech First have even legally challenged policies, such as the University of Michigan's policy that convenes a group of staff to focus on "addressing incidents that may reflect bias against members of the University community based on their identity."[4] This challenge to the policy was supported by the Department of Justice, which released a statement saying the University of Michigan's policy was unconstitutional.

Third, some people argue that seeing microaggressions everywhere and feeling that words can do violence actually feeds "victim culture" and makes people (especially young people) more fragile. This argument is captured in Greg Lukianoff and Jonathan Haidt's controversial book, *The Coddling of the American Mind*.[5] They argue that young people have been coddled—given trophies for "participation" by helicopter parents who don't think their children can handle disappointment.

After years of that shielding, those children now have an inability to cope with negative emotions generated from disappointment or even from ideas that they don't like. Lukianoff and Haidt further argue that young people see any ideas contrary to their own beliefs as a form of violence that needs to be limited or avoided. While the scientific argument about young people, and especially young women, having more anxiety and depression than before in recent history may be sound (and alarming), we take issue with the idea that sensitivity to subtle injustices is causing this problem and creating fragile young people.

There is empirical evidence that experiencing microaggressions takes a toll on people's emotional well-being and physical health.[6] However, there is no empirical evidence that we could find demonstrating that if people were ignorant of the microaggressions around them, they would be happier. And we're not quite sure what the practical advice that would stem from that finding would even look like. "Hey kids, bury your head in the sand to the injustice around you and you'll be happier"? We'd rather work toward trying to stop the microaggressions from happening in the first place.

And finally, others would argue that there is little scientific rigor or evidence to prove microaggressions exist and what harm they cause in the world. People would see this lack of evidence and quantitative rigor as reason to give less importance to the concept. If we can't measure it and prove it, it can't form the basis for policy. Scott Lilienfeld, a professor of psychology at Emory University, writes, for example, that the concept of microaggressions cannot be adequately defined and measured or shown to have an adverse effect on health.

As such, he calls for abandoning the term "microaggression" and for "a moratorium on microaggression training programs and publicly distributed microaggression lists pending research to address the [microaggression research program's] scientific limitations."[7]

The authors of this book both agree and disagree with some of these arguments. We do find the current climate in which it is hard to talk about sensitive issues problematic. We do want to find a way to create a culture where people can openly discuss sensitive topics, thinking more about the underlying concepts and feelings and less about the specific words that people use. However, we also agree that the subtle ways that verbal and nonverbal acts serve to exclude people have real and serious consequences, both in the moment and cumulatively.

We don't think that the fact that we can't boil all the subtle acts of exclusion down into one scientifically tight concept called "micro-aggressions" is a limitation that should stop us from addressing the range of SAE in practice. Our goal in this book is to offer a model of understanding and intervening on microaggressions that bridges the divide across polarized opinions about the concept of microaggressions itself. We think SAE can be talked about in a more open, civil way that brings people together rather than tearing people apart.

We believe that subtle acts of exclusion are a big problem and a big reason why we have not seen more progress in creating a more just and equitable society. The reason lies partly in that idea of "exclusion," and its opposite, "inclusion." Inclusion happens when people feel valued, respected, and part of a group. It's used regularly in the corporate world as a key concept. When employees feel included in the organization, not only are they happier and more satisfied (which is good in itself), but they also are more productive and efficient at their jobs, are better collaborators, and stay at the company longer. This has clear implications for an organization's bottom line, and research shows that more inclusive companies are also more profit-able than their less inclusive counterparts.[8] For all these reasons, SAE are a big deal.

When people feel excluded, the opposite is true. People may "phone it in" at their jobs, and they may even look for a different job. One of the most critical aspects of inclusion is that it must happen actively. When we just passively think of ourselves as good people but don't do anything to actively include others, that creates passive exclusion. There are specific inclusive behaviors that everyone at an organization can learn and practice that work to create a more inclusive environment and culture at the company.

Inclusion and exclusion can happen not just in organizations, but in specific social settings or even in cultures at large. To take the example from the book's introduction, if an African American man finds that people are consistently surprised that he can say something smart, over time, he may feel less as if people value and respect him and may feel excluded from mainstream culture. Or to take another example, if children of any demographic feel less included in schools, they are less engaged and have worse outcomes than those who feel enveloped in an atmosphere that cares for them and values them.

Subtle acts of exclusion, because they serve to diminish people, are critical to understand, identify, and address. We think there is a growing consciousness among many people, including many young people, about these subtle issues, and that, overall, is a good thing. But we need to be intentional about the way that those issues are discussed if we are to make real progress.

While having our eyes open to these subtle exclusions may not be as good for our happiness as being blissfully unaware of them, we think that's an OK trade-off. We find plenty of social science evidence for the existence of these subtle exclusions and the consequences and repercussions of them in big and small ways. As such, rather than abandoning the concept of microaggressions, we chose to improve it, and in this book we do that by reimagining the concept, adding clarity, and proposing systems for addressing the microaggressions using a practical and concrete approach.

Why Reframe the Term "Microaggression"?

The rest of the book will be dedicated to building an understanding around the subtle acts of exclusion that people have often called microaggressions, but we first want to explain why we hope to phase out that term eventually. We find that there are two main drawbacks to this term. First, as mentioned previously, there is a lack of clarity about what microaggressions are and why they are a problem. While the term itself is becoming better known, the majority of people have not heard the term. Even those who have heard the term still do not understand the concept well. If the only problem, however, was that people just hadn't heard the term "microaggression" or hadn't heard what it meant, that wouldn't be such a big deal. We'd just say, "Hey, let's get the word out about microaggressions!" But there is a more serious problem with this term itself.

The way the term frames the issue is not helpful at all for bringing people together and helping them work on solutions. What does it mean to say the way it "frames the issue"? Terms like "microaggressions" communicate implicit, unspoken messages that are often beyond our control. We may be trying to communicate about the importance of microaggressions, but the term itself is communicating implicitly that it's not really a big deal (just micro).

From a framing perspective, the term microaggressions is problematic in three ways. First, imagine that you have just unintentionally said something that offended someone because of their sexuality, and they say, "Can I talk to you about that microaggression?" The term itself provokes defensiveness. "I was not trying to be aggressive at all!" is most people's first reaction. When we examine how these interactions can be handled well, defensiveness is the enemy. It stops any progress before the interaction even gets started. And the term puts people on guard by focusing on the intent as aggressive. During the course of our diversity and inclusion workshops and keynotes, we have seen that defensive reaction again and again as we tried to talk about this concept.

Second, if I was the person who was offended, the term alienates me too—by communicating that this is only a small (micro) problem. What's the big deal, if it's just a microaggression? The term itself excludes people, making their concerns feel small and unimportant when what we want is the exact opposite of that.

Finally, by communicating that the whole issue is "micro," it lets everyone know that this is not something very important. Sure, we can talk about it, but it's less important than the other topics we will address. Our previous discussion on exclusion and the following discussion on SAE specifically make clear that these issues are not micro, but extremely important—to individuals who experience them and to all of us who hope for more equitable, inclusive spaces to live, work, and play in. The issues here deserve a new term—one that clarifies rather than confuses and brings people into a civil discussion rather than alienating them.

SAE Defined: Anatomy of an SAE

We propose a new term, subtle acts of exclusion (SAE). Though perhaps not as catchy as "microaggressions," we believe the term is much more useful because it clearly names and describes the phenomenon we are talking about. Here's how:

1. **They are subtle.** There is a wide range of acts that can insult, exclude, and harm. Many of these are obvious, and not covered in detail in this book, but many are in fact quite subtle. By calling them subtle we hope to shed light on the fact that they can be confusing, hard to identify, and challenging to speak about. We also recognize that while some of these exclusions may feel subtle to some, they may feel obvious to others, especially those who experience them again and again.

   It's important to recognize that we're not just talking about one thing, but a whole range of interactions that can vary in seriousness and in obviousness. The subtlety of some of them can also feed into "attributional ambiguity"—the sense of anxiety created when someone with a marginalized identity is unable to discern whether something happened because of said identity or some other random factors. In this book, we will discuss the wide variety of SAE. Examples we describe will range from short, quick interactions to more substantive stories with more context and exploration.

2. **They are acts.** They are things that people say and do. We don't know what someone's intention was in the moment, and so the term does not make assumptions about that or focus attention on that. As such, it doesn't provoke defensiveness the way microaggressions does. By focusing on SAE as acts, the term also attempts to avoid people feeling as if their character is being judged when they initiate an SAE. Because we're just talking about things people say and do, we can talk about why those particular things might have been a problem. And we can get better at not doing those things.

3. **They serve to exclude.** Finally, the term itself names the problem—that the subtle acts create exclusion rather than inclusion. This is a problem for that individual person who is being excluded in the moment. It is also a problem for the larger culture where the repetition of these SAE reinforces and maintains systems of power, inequality, bias, and what is considered normal.

Although we focus on SAE in this book, there are certainly other forms of exclusion and discrimination in the world. Other types of exclusion may include *explicit, intentional acts of exclusion* and *structural exclusion/inequality*. Explicit acts of exclusion would be things that people do purposely to exclude, including acts that can be objectively labeled as racist, sexist, hate crimes, intimidation, etc.

Structural exclusion is also more challenging to see because it is encoded into laws and policies. A classic example is how the minimum sentence for crack cocaine has been much greater than for powdered cocaine, though they are the same substance. Because crack cocaine was more of a problem in historically African American areas of cities, the difference in minimum sentencing created a disparity in prison time and a legal way that inequalities between racial groups were maintained.

With the obvious harm being done by explicit and structural exclusion, one might wonder why we have decided to focus on subtle acts of exclusion. We have chosen to focus on SAE for several reasons. First, because in the workplace, SAE are extremely common but can be difficult to recognize, especially for those who do not consistently experience them. Explicit acts of exclusion are easily identified and addressed, but SAE are still often a mystery to those who hope to improve workplace culture and foster more inclusion. Because SAE are often hard to recognize, they are also challenging to speak up about, and people often do not respond to them.

Additionally, we believe that SAE can often be addressed productively by those people directly involved in the moment. As such, we find that a book that can serve as a guide to help navigate the complexity of those interactions can be extremely useful. Finally, we find SAE to be particularly devious because of the way people can easily deny harm and because of the way they are often framed as just an individual insulting or offending another individual. Subtle acts of exclusion serve insidiously to reinforce bias (including unconscious bias) and subtle systems of power and hegemony (fancy word that means dominance and control but by cultural ideas rather than by direct violence). Subtle acts of exclusion need deep understanding, and we aim to bring it.

In this book, we focus much attention on workplaces. Inclusion and belonging are critical elements of effective workplaces, and organizations are beginning to understand that more and more. Organizations have a unique potential to make change by requiring or recommending wholesale adoption of the awareness and guidelines described in this book in an intentional way. However, this book can be used by anyone to improve inclusion in any context—in schools, in medical facilities, on sports teams, and with friends and family in everyday life.

As a key component to building deep understanding around SAE, we set out to develop a framework, or taxonomy, for identifying what each SAE was implicitly communicating. For example, when someone asks a Filipino man, "So, like—what are you?" on the surface they are just being curious and asking a question. However, implicitly, under the surface, they are communicating, "You are not normal," or "You are a curiosity."

We systematically thought about all the examples of SAE that we had heard about during interviews, experienced ourselves, observed, read about, and studied. We looked across them all and came up with a concise framework for SAE that covers the wide range that exists. Subtle acts of exclusion communicate these implicit messages to the recipient and to everyone around. Identifying the type of SAE and how it is serving to exclude can be helpful for being able to speak up about it.

The framework provides us with a language for describing why a particular SAE is a problem. You said one thing, but what you were implicitly communicating to me was something quite different. Many SAE can be communicating multiple types of exclusion at the same time. Yet we feel that this list accounts for the wide range of SAE that we examined across many different dimensions of diversity (gender, sexuality, race, ethnicity, age, disability, and religion).

FRAMEWORK OF SAE TYPES:

- You are invisible.
- You (or people like you) are inadequate.
- You are not an individual.
- You don't belong.
- You are not normal.

- You are a curiosity.
- You are a threat.
- You are a burden.

As mentioned, SAE often happen when people are trying to be good people. They slip out when people have good intentions, trying to

- compliment: "You're so professional,"
- be curious: "Where are you *really* from?"
- show comfort: "You're from Jamaica? I love Bob Marley!" and
- be funny: "Can we get el mucho discounto?"

One of the reasons it's so easy for SAE to slip out when people have good or benign intentions is that we all have unconscious (or implicit) biases. These are associations, assumptions, and expectations that we hold about certain groups of people without even necessarily being aware of it. Most people explicitly would *say* that boys and girls have equal potential to excel in science and math. And yet, researchers can demonstrate that the brain is subconsciously thinking something different from that. That unconscious bias can lead to all sorts of problematic decisions, behaviors, and subtle acts of exclusion.

Much has been written about the science of unconscious biases[9] as well as their implications for work and everyday life.[10] In this book, we focus on the resulting SAE and what to do about it, with the aspiration that addressing the SAE will not only impact observable behaviors but also the underlying bias itself.

Our recommendations for improving how we discuss SAE and for reducing their occurrence in the long run are based on deep understanding and simple guidelines rather than memorizing a list or surface-level scripts. The main idea is that we want people to be comfortable discussing SAE in a productive way when they happen. We encourage people to practice doing that, and in this book we give examples throughout of how to put these principles into action.

To describe the recommendations, we need a common language for talking about the actors in each scenario where SAE are happening.

- Let's call the person or group that is excluded by the SAE the **subject**. The subject can be present when the SAE happens, or might not be.

- Let's call the person who says or who nonverbally does the SAE the **initiator**.

- Anyone who overhears or sees the SAE will be called an **observer**. An observer has a very important role and is highly encouraged to speak up. In fact, an observer can shift from an observer to an ally by addressing the SAE through the process described in the following chapters.

- Once an observer speaks up, they become an **ally**.

- An observer who chooses not to speak up is a **bystander**.

This observer role is especially important, as it can take some of the burden off the SAE subjects, who may face significant repercussions for speaking up about SAE when they happen. African American women, for example, risk being stereotyped as "the angry Black woman" when they speak up about SAE that happen. Having an ally speak up can at least spread some of that burden around. That being said, observers may feel that it is not their place to speak up if they weren't the subject of the subtle act of exclusion. And sometimes, that may be true. Each situation is extremely complex, with many factors to consider. There is not one right way to handle every situation. But in general, this book aims to contribute to the discussion of what it means to be an ally. An ally is not someone you can be by just supporting people in your head. It requires a certain kind of everyday activism that includes speaking up when you observe SAE. If we all take responsibility, we can make much more progress together than if we wait for offenses to happen only to us before speaking up.

   In the following three chapters, we describe in more detail what to do to reduce SAE and to speak up about them when they happen. We describe what individuals can do and also what people in organizations can do to support these efforts. Then, in chapters 5 through 9, we delve deeper into some (not all) of the dimensions along which SAE commonly occur. We give real life examples from scenes we have witnessed or stories that people have told us. We acknowledge that these issues are incredibly complicated, that each SAE situation is unique. Nonetheless, we invite you to lean into the complexity and explore with us.

2

Personal Pre-Work: Beyond Inactive Bystanders

NOW THAT WE HAVE DEFINED what subtle acts of exclusion are, what do you do when it happens to you? Whether you are the initiator, the subject, or the observer, the first thing to do is be prepared. If you have already been on the receiving end of microaggressions, you have probably felt the startling upset that accompanies them. Part of the reason SAE are so jarring is that to the receiver, they are typically out of the blue and inappropriate. If you are the SAE initiator, you most likely remained unphased by the microaggression . . . until someone spoke up.

The first step in being prepared is to connect with the marginalized parts of your own identity. As the multiple minority coauthor, Jana has had quite a bit of experience with microaggressions. The perspectives they share often exemplify the challenges of intersectionality—or the overlapping systems of discrimination and bias present for a person of multiple marginalized identities.

> I used to frequently be approached by people in stores looking for help finding items. There was something about me that read

"employee" versus "patron." I will never forget the last time I was in an American Girl store shopping for my daughter. I was looking for the matching doll dress for the Easter dress I had just pulled off the rack when another customer jumped in front of me asking for a dress in a different size. She assumed I was an employee. Interestingly, she wasn't even looking for context clues, like the fact that I had on a coat, or the fact that I was also carrying a handbag. The startling truth is that every single other shopper in that high-end toy store was white. There were a few other Black people in the store, but they were employees. I wouldn't have noticed because there were plenty of white employees, but I was wondering what it might have been about me that made this woman come to me for customer service. I was shopping just as she was. My skin color was the only thing I was left thinking could have been the reason.

Coauthor Jana talked about attributional ambiguity in their previous books *Overcoming Bias: Building Authentic Relationships across Differences* and *Erasing Institutional Bias: How to Create Systemic Change for Organizational Inclusion*. Attributional ambiguity, as mentioned in the previous chapter, is when someone with a marginalized identity doesn't know whether something happened because of that identity or something else. It's often impossible to know which marginalized identity, if any, is playing a role in the microaggression, though we hope that the framework of different types of SAE described in the previous chapter can help disentangle the complexity.

In the case of Jana's story, it could have been any number of other factors, but the pattern repeats itself in their life persistently. Jana explains,

Employees at Target wear khakis and red shirts, yet if I had a dollar for every distracted Target shopper who asked me a customer service question or the more direct query, "Do you work here?" I would probably have enough for a cross country road trip. Maybe it's because I look like a nice person, or because sometimes I present female. Maybe it's because I smile and say hello when I pass people. Whatever the case, it's exhausting and annoying and it makes me wish folks would focus and see people as individuals before making assumptions. This is an example of stereotyped assumptions. For whatever reason, maybe race or gender, people assume I fit in a service role rather than the role of customer, like them.

This is a relatively benign example. There are no life or death consequences being described. That's why these were originally called *micro*aggressions. The challenge is that when we stack these experiences on top of each other, the weight becomes crushing for those of us experiencing them day after day, in terms of physical, mental, and emotional well-being. In the next section, we will invite you to connect with your own marginalized identities and experiences.

Some readers may not have obvious marginalized identities that come to mind, like coauthor Baran, who is a heterosexual white male. People in Target are not asking if he works there. People are not asking to touch his hair. But that doesn't mean he hasn't experienced marginalization along other dimensions of identity in different ways. He is Jewish, for example, and experiences frequent SAE based on religious dimensions. And he has lived many years in countries other than the United States, where he grew up. In fact, that experience of living outside one's own "home" culture is one of the foundational pieces of training to be a cultural anthropologist.

Sometimes the "normalness" of being in the majority in a place makes it hard to spot the SAE that continuously happen to others, and that experience of no longer being part of the majority allows a person to recognize subtle cultural exclusions and their implications in a new way, even after they return to their "own" culture. In the case of Baran, those experiences were critical for opening his eyes to the fact that SAE were happening to others around him all the time.

Those experiences also helped him open his heart and ears to listening deeply to others and what they were experiencing. Not everyone can go live for two years in a different culture, but everyone can open themselves up to new and different experiences that take them out of their comfort zones.

Recognize that your own way of thinking about the world comes from your unique experiences and take time to listen to others on their own terms. Diversify your experiences and your networks. Ask questions. You can even ask people, as Baran did during interviews with people on the street, "Have you ever experienced subtle things at work that made you feel disrespected, undervalued, or as if you didn't belong?" Just asking the question and listening to those answers can be illuminating.

If you are struggling to think of a marginalized identity that forms part of you, this book will be especially useful for you. This first part of connecting with your own marginalized identity may be more challenging, but the detailed examples we provide will allow you to better understand and empathize with what others may experience. And we encourage you to push yourself in this section. Have you ever felt excluded? If so, why? What happened to make you feel that way? What was that experience like for you? What about in your past, did you ever feel excluded at any point growing up?

Many of us experienced bullying in middle school, for instance. Both authors currently have middle schoolers who are in the throes of arguably the most challenging stage of human interpersonal development. Bullying may seem petty and small on the surface, but many of us know from personal experience or from stories in the news and in our communities that it can wreak havoc on our self-esteem. The persistent, insidious nature of bullying is causing far too many young people to take their own lives. In this way, SAE, like bullying, can have detrimental effects. Human mental and emotional well-being can be tenuous. We must learn to handle ourselves and others with greater care.

Once you have connected to your own marginalized identities and/or experiences, you will be more empathetic toward people you inadvertently commit SAE against. If you are the initiator and someone speaks up and calls you out, remember your own experience and listen for understanding. Remember that SAE can be committed by anyone depending on context, even those that are from marginalized backgrounds. This is *shared* work we are asking us all to engage in.

Connect with Your Own Marginalized Identities

The fastest way to understand the impact of microaggressions is to identify with the ones that have affected you. Fair warning: the more marginalized identities you have, the easier this part of the exercise will be. By "marginalized identities" we mean the parts of who you are that are legally protected by, for instance, Title VII laws in the United States (race, sex, religion, age, etc.) or any identity dimension that causes large parts of society to treat you as "less than," or like a second-class citizen, unequal to others. Groups who are in the minority often have disproportionately frequent experiences with subtle acts of exclusion. Some of these demographics can include but are not limited to the following:

- people who are differently abled
- racial and ethnic minorities
- gender minorities (women, trans, gender fluid, gender non-conforming, etc.)
- foreigners living away from home nations
- queer people

If you do not identify with any historically marginalized identity, you may have to dig deeper. Maybe your family was less affluent than your peers' families growing up. Perhaps you are a first-generation college student, or a single parent. Some of these identities mirror the types of things people are bullied about in school. If you were ever bullied in school or anywhere else, you can draw on those experiences.

If you cannot find any marginalized group to identify with, you may be operating with a degree of privilege that makes it harder to connect to marginalized people's experiences. Whatever the case, any experiences where people have made assumptions about you, stereotyped you, or treated you with less dignity than you deserved will all be helpful on your understanding-SAE journey. A dearth of any such experiences may enable detached and uninformed behavior and attitudes about this subject matter, and thereby be all the more challenging and necessary for you to explore.

Now think about what was said or done to make you feel less than dignified. As you connect to that moment, remember that we never want to engage in what we call "oppression Olympics." Try not to compare your pain to anyone else's. All oppression hurts. We all arrive at each moment differently equipped to handle it. For this exercise, we want you to experience your own feelings and try to name them. Write down the marginalized identity (even if it doesn't fit neatly into a Title VII or other historically marginalized category—if you felt marginalized, that is sufficient). Then write down what was said or done followed by how it made you feel. Once you have your list of feelings, if they are not positive, reframe them as positive affirmations. The purpose of the reframe is to help you begin to rewire any old scripts that would cause you to internalize any marginalization.

Listen for Understanding

Once you have spoken up and addressed the problematic behavior, or worse, someone has called out *your* behavior—then it is time to listen. If you are the person who has made someone else aware of an SAE they might have committed, you need to stop and listen for understanding. The natural human reaction to being confronted in this way will be some form of defensiveness. Some people will be downright angry, others will be profusely apologetic, and others will just dismiss you and your unwanted criticism. Regardless of the response, you must quiet yourself and get out of the way of the exchange that may follow.

If your ego is involved in the exchange, it is far more likely to escalate into a shallow verbal altercation. You need to be prepared not to take whatever comes next personally. The person you approached will likely fall into their limbic brain and not think rationally for a short time. And if you were the initiator, just listen, stay calm, and try to remain as objective as possible. Being called out will likely trigger an emotional, defensive response. So this is the time to lean into the various mechanisms that people use to remain calm:

- ‣ Take a deep breath.
- ‣ Count to ten.
- ‣ Find an appropriate opening to ask for a minute and take a short walk.

Spend your mental energy listening and trying to understand the speaker's perspective instead of trying to formulate a response or a defense. If your brain has dropped into fight or flight mode, you won't be able to access your rational mind and you will likely make the situation worse if you speak up too soon.

If you choose to take a walk or otherwise collect yourself, make sure you do it with grace. Avoid storming out, leaving without words, or saying anything passive aggressive. We find that an affirming statement preceding a departure is useful. Something like, "I hear what you are saying and I would like to take a moment to process it," or "Thank you for bringing this to my attention. Can I go reflect on this and get back to you?" If you say you will come back to it, make sure to really come back to it.

We understand that it requires a healthy dose of humility to summon the courage to speak these words. But remember, if someone has called out your behavior and identified something you have said as a microaggression, they too mustered courage to name the subtle act of exclusion. And they or someone else has likely been adversely affected by what was said.

It's OK to be nervous about speaking up when you witness a subtle act of exclusion. There is a great video on YouTube from Burger King that shows how adults are still uncomfortable speaking up against bullying (see activity 1).

ACTIVITY 1

Go to the link or Google "Whopper Jr Bullying" and watch the video.

https://www.youtube.com/watch?v=mnKPEsbTo9s

Follow-up questions:

- How did the video make you feel?
- How do you think the target felt?
- What do you think the bystanders were thinking?

This is not a video on subtle acts of exclusion—these acts were overt and aggressive. The point is that even when faced with children bullying other children, which most people will agree is unkind and unacceptable, we still struggle to speak up. We felt this book was needed to help people have the tools and the confidence to do the hard thing in service of community.

This is why it is important for us to connect with our own stories and experiences of marginalization. It is far easier to connect with someone else when we can relate. Again, we should avoid comparing our pain to anyone else's, but leveraging our own pain in service of building connection and understanding is a good thing. Remember that it is hard to think straight when your defenses are triggered. Having someone else step up for you can be an emotional life saver. Not everyone wants people to come to the rescue during SAE, but it's certainly better to offer support than to sit idly by and watch your fellow human suffer even the smallest slight.

From Observer to Ally

Coauthor Dr. Jana recently presented a keynote to a group of 200 corporate employees.

> A gentleman spoke into the microphone during the Q&A and framed a question in a way I had never been asked in any of my previous keynotes. He asked, "As a white man in corporate America, what can I do to help erase institutional bias when I am the beneficiary of privilege?" Needless to say, I was taken aback. I could tell the question was sincere. I immediately acknowledged the magnitude of his query (arguably ally behavior in itself). I told him that I had never had a white, cisgendered (expressed gender matching assigned gender at birth), male audience member simultaneously own his privilege while requesting guidance on how to address bias that benefits him.
>
> I publicly praised his choice and the room burst into applause. Contextually, his presence was already a bold statement. You see, the event was part of a women's empowerment series. Being in that room, as a man, was an expression of ally behavior. My response was for him to continue being a willful coconspirator. I encouraged him to be an ally and speak up when the opportunity presented itself—to stand for those whose voices aren't being heard. It's a delicate balance, to amplify marginalized voices without speaking over them. To ask where to serve instead of assuming you already know. And in the case of SAE, allyship is an open opportunity available to those who are ready and willing.

When you witness an SAE, you have choices. You can remain silent. You can gossip about it with others. Or you can help the initiator *and* the subject by naming the problematic behavior. Calling out SAE is the best way to foster an inclusive environment in which microaggressions are not welcomed. When you stand up for the subject of an SAE, you relieve them of the pressure of having to process the affront while confronting the initiator. In the following chapter, we give specific guidelines for what to do when an SAE occurs, and in this chapter we give some important overall considerations.

When confronting the initiator, do so with grace. Let them know what they said or did and why you perceived it as problematic. Then listen and wait for a response. If they are not showing signs of upset, feel free to proceed with helping them see the perspective of the SAE subject. If they are showing signs of distress, offer to speak with them at a later time in a more relaxed setting after they have had some time to process the data you presented.

The mere fact that some people are likely to devolve into more primal versions of themselves exposes why we should choose our moments and settings for educating people wisely. It is not always wise to challenge an SAE in a setting where the speaker will lose face. This is part of the reason your ego must be removed from the situation as much as possible. If you leverage an SAE callout moment to serve your own ego and embarrass your boss, a colleague, or someone you don't like or agree with, you are asking for trouble. Exposing an SAE should be a compassionate act of caring, designed to help another person stay in relationship with people they might otherwise inadvertently alienate. There should never be blaming, shaming, maligning, or intentionally embarrassing someone when calling out a microaggression. Again, this is why we prefer the term "subtle acts of exclusion."

Naming a microaggression tends to make people feel judged. When people feel judged, they are less willing, and likely less able, to learn and receive new information. The information may be incredibly useful and likely to increase their emotional intelligence and cultural fluency. Yet, if people feel judged, they will experience you as someone who thinks they are superior to them in some way. You immediately position yourself as the enemy. So listening to understand is critical. Allow the person to share their perspective, their confusion, or perhaps their hurt and embarrassment. Whatever they throw out next, be willing to listen with an empathetic ear and a steady heart. What they say may feel like an attack, but understand that what you said may feel that way to them as well. Breathe through it and try to be there with them, fully present, always communicating that you are on their side and wanting to help, not blame.

Now, you will also encounter people who are much more grounded, centered, and evolved—folks who can hear criticism without losing their cool. These are the people whose sense of personal integrity and identity are not so easily shaken—at least not by a single calling out of a sociocultural misstep. Those conversations will go much more smoothly, require less grit from you, and be marked by an expansion of trust and closeness. People who are open to constructive criticism offered in kindness and love will ask clarifying questions in search of greater understanding so they can avoid repeating the subtle act of exclusion. These are the conversations that make the effort worth it.

These encounters will give you life and help you feel that you are indeed part of the solution. The more angst-filled confrontations will also leave you feeling empowered. It just takes longer for those to resolve, and you both will have to process through so many complex emotions that you will be exhausted sometimes. Part of us doesn't want to tell you that. Part of us wants to say it will all go great and you won't have any battle scars whatsoever. But that would be untrue and unkind. You may lose friends, some forever, and some may come back around after they've licked their proverbial wounds. But our question is that, if we are not here to serve each other and to improve ourselves and help grow each other in loving, honest relationships—then why are we here? If you are here just to get as much out of life for yourself, other people's feelings and well-being be damned, then this is not the book for you.

Think before You Speak

If what you intend to say is about or to a marginalized person, it is worth asking yourself a few quick questions in advance. Think about the SAE taxonomy and whether you may be walking into one of those inadvertent exclusions. We realize that it may feel like an obtrusive and unnecessary burden to think before you speak. But if you consider the damage that a serious misstep can do to a career and to the affected lives, we believe the exercise is worthwhile.

- Is what I am about to say/ask based on stereotypes or assumptions about a marginalized group?

- Is what I am about to say/ask unnecessarily intrusive?

- Am I overstepping?

- Is what I am about to say based in kindness and generosity or the opposite?

- Do I have the authority/right to tell/ask this person to comply with my request?

- Is this a good use of my authority/privilege?

- Would I say the same thing to a person of a different gender/ color/race, etc.?

- Is this going to make the person feel inadequate or as if they don't belong?

- Does this question their normalcy or make them feel like a threat or a curiosity?

- Will this make someone feel invisible, as if they are not an individual?

A little bit of thought can go a long way toward disrupting some of the problematic patterns that we fall into when biased behaviors are left unchecked. This is why it is so important for us to speak up on behalf of ourselves and each other whenever possible. The best way for each of us to learn to do better is to have greater insight into the effect our behaviors have on the people around us. How can we improve if no one is brave enough to let us know that we have areas for improvement?

The difficult part that follows is the ability to receive critical feedback without taking it personally. We must note that it is not the SAE subject's responsibility to teach you about the offending subtle act of exclusion. If they choose to enlighten you, consider that a gift and an act of trust. It can be socially and professionally perilous, particularly for marginalized demographics, to speak up about subtle acts of exclusion. This is why it is imperative that observers become allies by speaking up and helping SAE initiators understand the problematic behavior. Listen for the answers to the questions listed previously in the feedback you do receive from allies and subjects of subtle acts of exclusion. They may reveal an opportunity to become more culturally competent.

If you received the feedback, closing the loop means remembering not to overreact when you are called out. It means recalling why this work is important and forgiving the messenger even if they don't handle it well. They may call you out in front of people or allow their egos and opinions to color the interaction in a way that feels diminishing. We ask that you take author Don Miguel Ruiz's sage advice from his book of Toltec wisdom *The Four Agreements*, and "don't take anything personally."[1] Listen to the message, not the messenger. Extract the useful parts and distill them into something that can influence your behavior for the better.

If you are the person who called out the SAE, then we believe you have a duty of care to the person you called out. (See activity 2.) We don't advise running around pointing out microaggressions willy-nilly and just leaving folks out to dry. One could argue that your pointing out the microaggression is a subtle act of exclusion. It can certainly feel that way to the recipient of your criticism, albeit constructive.

ACTIVITY 2

Think of a time when someone called you out for doing or saying something biased or inappropriate.

- How did you respond?

- What could they have done differently?

- What could you have done differently?

- How did the situation resolve?

- What did you learn from the situation?

Consider your responses to the activity questions as they will serve you should you ever find the need or opportunity to confront someone else's behavior. Firsthand memory of how it feels to be called out can help increase your empathetic response when the roles are reversed.

That said, in service of staying in community and in relationship, we suggest following up or at least taking the time to ensure that you have minimized any adverse impact on the individual. And of course, if the SAE subject was present for the misstep, do check in with them and communicate that you experienced the slight with them or alongside them. See whether they are OK. Ask if you can be there for them. See them and treat them with the dignity they deserve. Avoid pretending it never happened. This renders the subject invisible and silently condones the subtle act of exclusion. If you aspire to be an ally, that is the last thing you wish to convey.

Close the Loop

Coauthor Jana cites the following SAE as one of their most embarrassing life experiences:

> Earlier in my career when I spent much of my time in the training room, I found myself the initiator of an SAE. It was Take Our Daughters To Work Day, and my middle-school-aged daughter, now a junior at Harvard, attended an offsite training with me. It was an exciting day, as it was the first time she had ever experienced me in my training role. During one of the breaks, I noticed what I thought was a child wearing a shirt with the client logo on it and said, "Aww look! You're the tiniest little [client name] employee I've ever seen!" I said this with so much happiness and enthusiasm that the intent was probably clear . . . or so I thought.
>
> I continued to my destination and eventually shared with my cofacilitator that I think I may have just insulted an adult by assuming she was a child. I told him what had transpired. He laughed and said, indeed, I probably had. He advised that I just go find her and apologize. Mortified, I went to find her, and staring into the face of what appeared to be a nine-year-old child, I doubled down on failure and asked, "Are you a grown up?"
>
> . . .
>
> The look that her colleague gave me was all the answer I needed. I couldn't believe that I had just made a bad situation worse. What was I thinking? I wanted to die in that moment. I was literally trying to apologize and I insulted her *again*. Thankfully she had more grace than I did. She smiled and told me not to worry about it. She said she indeed was an adult and that it happens all the time. (If looks could kill, I would be a dead person because the colleague was still glaring at me and shaking her head

in utter disbelief.) Desperately seeking rationalization, I shared that my daughter was at work with me and that I somehow primed myself for seeing children at work that day. It was *my* company that had visiting children, not hers. Epic fail.

The two things that made that horrible situation bearable were (1) the graciousness of the subject. She was the victim of my SAE and owed me zero kindness. And (2) that my cofacilitator checked in on me after everything had transpired and again after the dust had settled. He wanted to make sure that I was OK because I had messed up and had tried to make it right. The first part was easy; the second part, not so much.

These conversations really are gifts that allow us to grow, learn, appreciate others, and build deeper connections. After one of these conversations, everyone involved could do some independent follow-up that might include reading a book, doing an internet search about the concepts discussed, reflecting and introspecting, or talking with trusted friends and family members. After that individual follow-up, share thoughts with the person you had the initial SAE conversation with. That shows them that you care and reinforces the productivity of these interactions.

3

Interpersonal Action: SAE Accountability

ONCE YOU HAVE DONE the preparation described in the previous chapter, you are ready to learn what to do when an SAE happens. We believe that there are many complex and sometimes competing factors that influence whether one chooses to speak up about SAE, especially in the workplace. However, we also believe that most often, if there is a possibility of a productive conversation without negative repercussions, the best course of action is to speak up. This chapter will describe some basic guidelines for best practices—speaking up in a way that holds people accountable with productive, open, and civil conversations. We call this the SAE accountability system.

We have distilled the basic guidelines down into action steps for speaking up for SAE accountability, depending on what role you played in the SAE interaction. Were you the initiator, the subject, or the observer? The following sections give some guidelines to follow depending on your specific role.

Please note that no matter what your role tends to be in SAE interactions, it will be helpful for you to read the guidelines for all three roles. That is, first, because you will sometimes find yourself in different roles, and so you should be familiar with all the guidelines. Second, it will help the interaction go smoother if you know what the expectations are for the other roles as well. One best practice is for organizations themselves to set the ground rules. This will be discussed in more depth in chapter 4. The basic idea is that organizations can set the conditions for these conversations to succeed by providing a common language, training, and practice for all leaders and employees so they can be on the same page. When everyone is on the same page for SAE accountability, the discussions can go much easier because people get in the habit of reacting in productive ways together—whether they are the initiators, the subjects, or the observers.

GUIDELINES FOR SPEAKING UP AS THE SAE SUBJECT OR OBSERVER:

1. Pause the action.

2. Assume good intent.

3. Explain why the action was paused.

4. Have patience but expect progress.

GUIDELINES FOR RESPONDING AS THE SAE INITIATOR:

1. Acknowledge the feedback with gratitude.

2. Replace defensiveness with curiosity and empathy.

3. Follow through and follow up.

Guidelines for Speaking Up as the Subject or Observer

In this section, we go into depth for each of the guidelines for SAE subjects and observers. While we acknowledge openly that following all these guidelines may not be possible every time, they do represent best practices for productive conversations that have tangible benefits. We have grouped the guidelines for the subject and the observer together because they will both be in the position of speaking up and giving feedback to the initiator. Where relevant, we describe slightly different nuances for those two roles.

Guideline 1: Pause the Action

The most critical guideline is pausing the action. Most SAE continue to occur because subjects and observers get stuck trying to figure out what to say, and by the time they have some ideas, the moment has passed and they just let it go. Or people spend some time trying to assess whether they have the emotional energy for turning a casual conversation into a very different kind of conversation, and again by the time they decide, the moment has passed. These are both reasonable deliberations that people have. First, it is hard to know what to say. That's the very nature of subtle acts of exclusion! Second, when speaking up about SAE, the initiator often reacts negatively. They often feel embarrassed or defensive. And subjects or observers are hesitant to give feedback, anticipating that negative reaction. Coauthor Baran often tells a story about one time he expected that it might not go so negatively:

> One time I was taking a yoga class. It's not something I regularly do (though I wish I did have the time to do it more!). The yoga instructor kept telling the class to really push the stretch, to really feel it, "to not gyp ourselves." She kept repeating that idea for ninety minutes—that we should not "gyp" ourselves, meaning that we shouldn't cheat ourselves, but should really give it full effort. You've all probably heard that word before in various contexts. People may say, "Don't gyp me," meaning "Don't cheat me" or "Don't short me." Most people don't know that the word comes from a derogatory way of referencing gypsies (itself considered a derogatory word by some). We don't hear the word "gypsy" much in the United States, and I really think people have no idea where it comes from.
>
> Nonetheless, it was really grating on me, so I decided to say something afterward to the yoga teacher. I gave a lot of context,

> saying, "There's something you were saying that I wanted to let you know about. It's something really obscure that I only know because I do diversity and inclusion work for a living. I'm sure no one else even noticed, and I'm sure you don't know this either. But this word, gyp, is historically a negative reference to a group of people, and maybe you could say something neutral like 'Don't cheat yourself' instead."
>
> Maybe it was the post-yoga endorphins, but I was sort of expecting that at least in this one particular context, my speaking up would go really well. I figured she would say something like, "Wow, I had no idea. Thanks so much for bringing that up; sure won't say that again." And then we'd tell each other "namaste" or something like that and all would be well. Of course, that's not how it went. She didn't react aggressively or defensively, but she seemed mortified, avoided looking me in the eye, and as soon as possible just turned and walked out of the room. So it didn't feel good to me. But I bet she doesn't use that word anymore. And if we were coworkers, there would be more work we'd have to do together to make sure our working relationship remained intact.

Because most people are not diversity and inclusion experts like the authors, it's important to think of something simple that can be said to pause the action when an SAE happens. When an organization is training everyone in the SAE accountability system, everyone can agree ahead of time on something simple that people can say that simply pauses the action and signals that an SAE discussion is going to take place. We find that something very simple like, "Hold up," or "Hold on," or even "Pause" can be effective.

When everyone is agreed on the same word, it can be especially effective. For example, author and diversity and inclusion consultant Leslie Aguilar suggests that people speak up by using something as simple as "Ouch."[1] Coauthor Baran has suggested to some small organizations that they say "Yellow card," using the metaphor of a yellow card in soccer as a way to enter these conversations. These can work when everyone is trained on what to say, because they are a little unusual in everyday conversation. When you are just an individual following the guidelines without institutional support, you'll need to choose something more immediately understandable, like "Hold on."

No matter what you decide as an individual, a facilitator, or an organization, make it something that people will be able to say right in the moment, before they realize what they even want to say about it. Finally, it is also important to note that *anyone* can pause the action. It could be the subject of the SAE, the observer, or even the initiator. The authors have seen cases where as soon as the words leave someone's mouth, they realize it was not a good thing to say and they stop the action themselves.

Coauthor Baran found himself doing that, calling himself out, while facilitating a workshop on unconscious bias:

> During the discussion, a white person was telling a story about their also-white boss who used the N-word during a meeting they were having. I asked, "Was that the first time he did it?" And as soon as it left my mouth, I realized that I had assumed that the offender was male. In my head, I think it was less because of unconscious bias that the boss would necessarily be male and more of an assumption that a male would be more likely to use the N-word. Either way, it wasn't right, and I called it right out in front of the workshop. By doing that, I was inadvertently able to underscore the point I was trying to make that all of us have unconscious bias and all of us say things we shouldn't!

Observers, in particular, may feel hesitant to pause the action because they may feel as if they are not directly involved. The SAE was not directed at them, and they may feel as though it's none of their business. We want to underscore the point mentioned earlier in the book that observers play a key role in speaking up about SAE and becoming allies. Observers might want to give some context when they do speak up to explain to both the initiator and the subject why they are speaking up. They could say something like, "Hi, this might sound strange coming from me. I know you weren't even talking to me and that I wasn't really involved in that interaction. But I overheard, and I am following a system where I speak up every time I hear something that feels as if it might be excluding someone." Then observers can follow the rest of the guidelines.

Guideline 2: Assume Good Intent

For better or worse, we live in a culture that is largely "call out" rather than "call in."[2] People point out things that others do and say while also implying that the offender is essentially a racist/sexist/homophobe or, at the least, uncaring and potentially ignorant. Some have called this a "toxic call-out culture" in which people almost compete to demonstrate to others how woke they are.[3] They make others feel bad and stupid for not knowing that certain things are wrong. They do not assume good intent.

While we can appreciate that people are often fed up with SAE and other injustices and that there are times when a strong call-out is exactly what is needed, we find that for the most part, the call-out culture is not a productive way to go about things, especially in the workplace. In the first place, we all have unconscious bias of some sort. That doesn't make us bad people, it makes us human. That's important for people to remember as they call out biases in other people. And in the second place, calling someone out as a bad person is unproductive for pointing out a specific action that person took, helping them understand why it was a problem, and really improving that person's future behavior. As such, we prefer to think of speaking up in terms of "calling people in" to a conversation.

The majority of people want to be good people and have good intentions. Coauthor Jana likes to add levity to this idea by asking the groups they facilitate, "Who came here today with the goal of pissing people off on purpose?" And inviting people to raise their hands by throwing a hand up first. Sometimes folks will jokingly play along and raise their hands, thereby extending the joke. Jana subsequently summarizes the intent of the bit by pointing out that none of us really woke up that day hoping to rub people the wrong way. Then people are invited to remember the thought exercise as the day moves on and asked to assume good intent if their peace is at any point disturbed.

Speaking up about SAE will go most productively if people assume good intent in others, whether it's the person who initiated the SAE or the observer or the subject. This applies to any situation, whether it's during a specific facilitation or just in one's daily life. As discussed previously, the SAE initiator will often feel attacked when someone pauses the action because of something they said or did. The subject or observer can try to put them at ease by saying things like, "I know you didn't mean anything by this," "I know you probably don't know," "I know you were just trying to be curious." Assuming good intent and talking about things people *did* or *said* rather than their *character* is critical for more productive conversations. When we assume that people's characters are fundamentally good and that their intents are also good, we can have discussions that aren't as threatening.

Guideline 3: Explain Why the Action Was Paused

After the action is paused with the simple phrase you have decided on, the person who paused it can explain why they did so. You may know exactly why you paused the action, because it's something you've experienced a lot, overheard a lot, or thought about a lot. Or you may not know exactly why you paused things, especially if you are an observer speaking up as an ally. If you are the subject of the SAE, it may be that the SAE made you feel bad. You can explain why it made you feel bad using the framework described in chapter 1. Hopefully that gives you even more clear words to use to explain what the SAE implicitly communicated to you. For example, you could say, "I know you didn't mean it, but when you asked where I was really from, it made me feel as if I didn't belong here."

If you are attempting to speak up as an ally, it's more complicated because it might not have made you personally feel undervalued, and you may not know if the SAE made the other person feel as bad as you think it did. As such, you may qualify what you say: "I know you didn't mean it that way, and I'm not even sure if X person interpreted it that way, but it sounds to me as though it's subtly communicating that that person is not normal."

It may be that the SAE has made an assumption that shouldn't have been made. It may be that the person who spoke up doesn't really know why the SAE was a problem but something just didn't feel right about it. Those cases provide excellent opportunities for calling people in. You may say something like, "Hold up. I know you didn't mean anything bad by that, but something about it doesn't feel quite right. Can we think about this together?"

Guideline 4: Have Patience but Expect Progress

We want to acknowledge that we are asking a lot of people when they speak up. We are asking you to start what is bound to be a difficult conversation. We are also asking you to open yourself up for potential negative repercussions. And we are asking you to keep a level head about it when it is likely something that is extremely personal and emotional. That can be one of the most challenging aspects to following these guidelines. You might have the same SAE happen to you dozens (or hundreds!) of times. It keeps happening, and you may be sick of it. Yet, the latest initiator might never have gotten the feedback that what they said was a problem.

Because SAE conversations can be sensitive and emotional, you also must be in tune with your own readiness for the conversation. As the subject, especially, you may find that you are not in an emotional state that allows for an SAE discussion. That is extremely common, especially as you have these conversations perhaps for the first time. If that is the case, don't be afraid to ask for the time you need. For example, if you were the subject of the SAE and you speak up about it, you may be understandably upset. You might want to say, "Hold up. I know you didn't mean it like this, but what you just said really upset me. I need a little time to get to a place where I can discuss it with you. Can we meet for coffee tomorrow?" This allows the person who speaks up to be able to have patience with that initiator, which is important for productive conversations.

Patience, however, only lasts so long. When we give that initiator the gift of feedback, we expect progress in return. We don't expect them to get everything right 100 percent of the time, but we do expect that they will follow their own guidelines and we expect that they will make an effort to improve their behavior around that SAE. If that progress is not made, especially at work, you may justifiably have to escalate the feedback to an HR department or some agreed-upon third party.

Guidelines for Responding as the SAE Initiator

In the following section we provide guidelines for the person who says or does the subtle act of exclusion. We have all played this role at some point in our lives. When it next happens to you (and it will), if you follow the guidelines, you will find that you have a great deal of agency to make the interaction go well. It's not easy, but it can be incredibly gratifying.

Guideline 1: Acknowledge the Feedback with Gratitude

If you are the person that said or did the SAE, it's helpful to see someone giving you feedback as a wonderful chance to improve your behaviors around inclusion. That person has given you a gift. They spoke up, even though it was hard, in an effort for you both to make the world a better place. Conversations like these and feedback like this provide us all with opportunities to grow, to know more about our coworkers, and to create more inclusion for the organization.

It's helpful to explicitly acknowledge the discussion with gratitude. The subject or observer may feel worried that they are going to be perceived as stirring up trouble or being too sensitive. They can be put at ease by the initiator, who might say something like, "Thank you so much for speaking up about this." You may be thinking that this will come across as fake, because deep down you are embarrassed or feel defensive. However, if you get in the mindset of gratitude and get in the practice of acknowledging even critical feedback like this, it can really start to feel natural and the appreciation can be genuine.

Guideline 2: Replace Defensiveness with Curiosity and Empathy

Recall that when people speak up about SAE that occurred, they are trying to help us improve and be even more inclusive. They are not trying to call us out to make us feel bad. In that spirit, we should approach those conversations as opportunities to learn rather than feeling the need to defend. And it's critical to underscore that *SAE are never about intent*. That bears repeating. *SAE are never about intent*. So if you find yourself getting feedback about something you did, you should not try to clarify your intent (which is assumed to be good). Instead, listen to what the other person is saying and think about the impact that it had on them.

As described previously, when people are busy defending their own actions, it is much more difficult for them to truly hear someone else. We recognize that defensiveness is a common reaction to being called out for an SAE and that is why we prefer the language of calling in. Reacting non-defensively takes a lot of practice. The initiator of an SAE usually wants to explain their intent (to get to know the person, to be funny, to bond, etc.).

At this specific moment when the action has been paused, we train people to think about impact rather than intent. To truly hear the impact that an SAE might have caused, we have to be actively listening. That doesn't mean that there will always be acceptance of the observer's or subject's opinion. Disagreements sometimes happen. But in the moment when the SAE is first being discussed, all parties agree to not be defensive, and ideally they have practiced this reaction through trainings.

To approach the SAE conversation more productively, it's helpful to replace defensiveness with more positive mental states. Going into the conversation with curiosity about other people's experiences and empathy for their perspective is incredibly helpful. There are several simple practices that can help you actively listen without defensiveness. First, put yourself in a listening and learning mindset. If you are the person who initiated the SAE, your initial goal is not to explain anything about why you said it. Your only goal is to hear the other person.

Second, you can engage in simple behaviors to make the listening active and to help the other person feel heard. Consider any mix of the following:

- Ask follow-up questions, trying to better understand.

- Paraphrase what the other person is saying.

- Look the other person in the eye and make sure your body language is open.

- Refrain from interrupting and make sure that you are not looking at your cell phone or smartwatch. Seriously, if your phone is in your hand, put it in your pocket so you are not tempted.

- If your laptop is open, close it.

Research shows that those little gestures can make people feel more valued in your interactions with them.

If you were the person receiving feedback because you said something that was an SAE, realistically, you too might find yourself feeling too upset and defensive to have a good conversation about it.

In that case, you can say something like, "Thank you for speaking up about this. I'm feeling as though I am not going to be able to have a great conversation about this now. But it's really important to me. Can we come back to this tomorrow, maybe lunchtime?" If you say something like this, it's essential to really come back to it rather than using it as an excuse to put it off indefinitely.

There may be other times when you logistically just don't have the time for a conversation about subtle acts of exclusion. You may have a meeting coming up in a few minutes. You may have a big deliverable due soon. It's important that rather than trying to rush through a conversation in the moment, you schedule a time when you can devote your full attention to it. The benefit of taking this time to think is not only being more emotionally ready for the conversation or having the time to discuss, but also giving everyone a chance to do some research and talk to others and process their thoughts. It gives you a chance to think about what the other person is feeling and to really approach the conversation with empathy and gratitude.

When you can actively listen with enough time, it accomplishes two things. It helps you really understand better what the impact was of what you said. You can focus on that without worrying about how you are going to defend. But also, it makes the other person *feel* heard, which is critical for building inclusion. These active listening behaviors are great practice for any conversation, but for emotionally charged ones like those around SAE, they are essential.

Take some time and practice these skills during regular interactions with coworkers, family members, or friends. You will likely notice immediate results—that people feel great when you do it. Develop those habits with low stakes interactions, and then you will be ready for the more challenging conversations.

Guideline 3: Follow Through and Follow Up

If you had to put off finishing the conversation, make sure to come back to it. It is more important than you think. If the SAE happened at work, it's easy to think circling back is not critical for the job, but building trust and inclusion is essential for collaboration and creating an inclusive culture, which have a direct impact on the core business objectives. Closing the loop on SAE is not just the right interpersonal thing to do but is also important for the job.

After the conversation is done, it's essential to follow through with what you heard. If someone told you that they prefer a different pronoun from the one you have been using, make sure you put in the effort to use the one they prefer. You don't have to get it right every time, but you must try and you must make progress getting better at it. If a deaf person speaking to you through a sign-language interpreter has told you it makes him feel bad when you look at the interpreter but not at him, then make the effort to do it differently next time. Value the feedback and adjust accordingly. People don't expect you to be perfect, but if they have put themselves out by giving you that feedback, they expect you to try.

In addition to trying to adjust your behavior, it is also important to explicitly follow up with everyone involved—subjects and observer(s). Ideally this would be done in person or by phone, as we all know it's difficult to ensure accurate interpretation of emotion through email or text. Email and text can be part of the follow-up strategy but should not be the only component. The follow up shows others that they are valued and that the relationship is important. It can be something as simple as, "Hey, again, I wanted to thank you for speaking up about [fill in the SAE blank]."

Throughout this chapter, we have alluded to the benefits of having productive conversations around subtle acts of exclusion. To summarize, we have seen that direct benefits include the following:

- **Increased feelings of inclusion for people with marginalized identities.** People will feel valued and heard when SAE are addressed in a productive way. That feeling is critical, not only for individual people's happiness and satisfaction, but also for workplace productivity.

- **More trust among everyone.** Trust is essential for teams to be high functioning. It makes it so that people are able to be vulnerable with one another, to communicate openly with one another, to ask for help when they need it, to offer critical feedback when that is needed, and so much more. And the benefits of building trust around SAE will transfer to build trusting relationships more broadly.

- **More collaboration across organizations.** When trust is built and inclusion is increased, organizations will truly be able to reap the benefits of diverse teams with increased collaboration.

- **Improved ability to give feedback on other issues.** When people practice SAE accountability and can give and receive feedback on some of the most challenging and sensitive issues, they also learn skills that help in giving feedback about other issues. This is critical for teams to achieve maximum performance.

- **A culture of transparency, interpersonal civility, and accountability.** Cultures can sometimes take on lives of their own. When a culture around SAE accountability is started, it can organically work to feed and foster a more productive culture in general.

The responsibility for having productive conversations like this falls on everyone, at work or outside of it, no matter which role you played in the subtle act of exclusion. Nonetheless, there are some institutional practices and policies that can support the conversations in a way that sets them up for success. In the following chapter, we will explain what can be done institutionally to move toward an overall "speak up" culture where people are open, honest, and trusting about these important issues.

4

Institutional Action: Embedding SAE Accountability

ORGANIZATIONAL LEADERS have a responsibility to keep people safe from psychological harm in the workplace. Employees have a legal right to work in a place free from harassment, including the hostility associated with an environment saturated with unaddressed subtle acts of exclusion. It is quite normal for SAE to happen in the workplace. It is the response from others, from HR, and from leadership that determines the outcome and whether they become an acceptable part of the organizational culture. Our goal is to help you identify ways to create an environment that is unwelcoming to SAE by creating accountability and naming the problem.

We have discussed how to prepare for speaking up about SAE (chapter 2) and how to most productively think about SAE conversations as individuals (chapter 3). The actual interventions are the same when they happen in institutions. The only difference is that the organization explicitly supports people speaking up about SAE by naming the dynamic and providing structural guidance on how to intervene. Institutions that *expect* people to speak up in the face of

SAE are inclusion leaders. These are the champions that are creating workplaces where people feel safe and supported.

Organizationally, our goal should be to cultivate an environment in which all people involved in an SAE (the initiator, the subject, and the observer) have practiced how to respond in a productive way. Organizations can lay the fertile ground for creating the conditions in which speaking up is productive by considering the following factors:

1. **Expect SAE to happen.** When people are working closely together, when they are pushing the boundaries of comfort to employ diverse teams, and even when they are trying their hardest to be inclusive, SAE are bound to happen. This is especially true when people are trying to have difficult conversations about sensitive topics, but SAE can happen anytime. Expecting them to happen, rather than being surprised and taken aback, is critical in order to be adequately prepared.

   Coauthor Baran thinks about this in terms of a helpful metaphor. He has a son who went to an amazing preschool where the young children repeated their values every day, and one of the values was "We make mistakes." That was part of their identity as students in that school. And the brilliance of having that as a value meant that the students were able to push themselves, challenge themselves, take risks, and really grow without feeling bad about mistakes. Similarly, if you make it part of your company culture to explicitly acknowledge that people are going to make mistakes, you can be prepared and handle them in a way that everyone grows and feels included.

   This kind of culture shift would support the idea of nurturing psychological safety within organizations. Leaders should be concerned with creating spaces that support the psychological and emotional well-being of their employees.

This includes the SAE subjects, observers, and even initiators. While it may be easier to understand the need to protect employees from the emotional harm caused by acts formerly known as microaggressions, people may not be as quick to protect those who we have identified as the initiators of the subtle acts of exclusion.

It is important to center everyone organizationally if we are to nurture a system of support, connection, and growth. There cannot be good guys, bad guys, and neutral bystanders. That is not a constructive paradigm. What we need to communicate is that it takes all of us to keep everyone safe. The very same person who is the subject of the SAE, or what others might consider the victim, might very well be the initiator on another occasion. Just as coauthor Jana highlights in their books *Overcoming Bias* and *Erasing Institutional Bias*—microaggressions, like bias, are part of the human experience. To be human is to unwittingly commit SAE from time to time. Our goal here is to raise your awareness enough that you can minimize the likelihood of committing them and empowered enough to intervene when you see them happening to yourself or others.

When you expect SAE to happen, it is easier to stay out of judgment. This way you can objectively intervene as needed. It is important not to sound accusatory and judgmental when the intervention takes place, because the initiator will likely feel defensive, as we explained in the previous chapter. Organizationally, the culture can normalize the act of intervening by helping people recalibrate their expectations that SAE are a common part of human behavior. It may seem counterintuitive to say, "Expect the thing you don't want," but this creates space for naming and for subsequent growth to take place.

Importantly, expecting SAE to happen does not give people a pass for continuing to commit them without trying to improve. Although we do not naively think that SAE will stop completely any time soon, we expect progress, and organizations should too.

2. **Communicate the norm.** When an organization adopts an accountability practice like this, everyone must be on board for it to function optimally, and contingencies must be planned for. For example, employees should know where to turn if speaking up does not go well or an SAE does not get resolved. An organization may decide to train people as allies or champions who are able to be neutral and assist with an SAE discussion, as some organizations are doing. People must also know how the SAE discussion will be escalated if it does not go well. That could mean taking the discussion to an HR representative who provides support. The guidelines for speaking up should be communicated clearly and also posted clearly as an easy reference.

This mechanism is a form of accountability. Accountability is precisely where most diversity-, equity-, and inclusion-related initiatives fail. Any organization can encourage leadership to talk about diversity and treating people with respect. Far too many will fail to implement actionable steps that embed accountability into the system. It is arguably more harmful to say you intend to protect people from harm—and then let them down—than to say nothing. Unfortunately, the status quo tends to mimic the childhood mantra "Sticks and stones may break my bones, but words will never hurt me." Managers often dismiss SAE altogether. They just don't see them as a big deal. Sometimes it's out of legitimate unawareness, and often it's because they simply lack the tools to intervene confidently.

Managers do not always know whether leadership will authentically support their efforts to stop subtle acts of exclusion. This is why the codification of anti-SAE policy and systematized procedures are useful. It's not about punishing people who slip up, it's about making room to name the problem and intervene in the moment to prevent further harm and the build up of accumulated animosity. Allowing SAE to remain unaddressed can create a festering in the hearts and minds of the people who tend to perpetually be subjected to them. Subtle acts of exclusion choke out people's freedom and sense of belonging.

For example, when a male employee is never stopped from cutting off women and gender nonbinary people in meetings, it becomes an irritating burden to the people who are always being interrupted. It becomes the status quo and those diverse voices eventually stop speaking up. In environments where SAE are never addressed, they accumulate so much around certain demographics that the subjects disengage and eventually leave the company for work somewhere that is more supportive and welcoming.

When organizations take the time to communicate the new norm and people are provided with the tools to make more informed choices, the atmosphere can be cleared of the stifling smog of incessant subtle acts of exclusion. This leads to a more inclusive and welcoming environment where all voices can feel a sense of belonging and the organization can thrive.

3. **Practice speaking up.** Because people's first response is often counterproductive, it takes practice to get that knee-jerk first response to be a more productive one. For example, the SAE initiator often responds defensively, which doesn't allow for productive discussions. It takes practice for all of us to not feel defensive when it is pointed out that we were the initiator of a subtle act of exclusion. Along the same lines, those who are the subject or the observer of an SAE sometimes have initial reactions that are unproductive as well, including reacting

angrily (understandable but not necessarily productive) or attacking a person's character rather than talking about the specific act ("You are a racist," "You are homophobic"). The practice can take many forms, including in-person training workshops and/or digital companions, ideally both. For a digital program on SAE that uses real people and scenarios such as those in this book to explore different possibilities of speaking up, check out *www.subtleactsofexclusion.com*.

Once the expectation is established that SAE will occur, and you have communicated the norm, the interventions should not come as a surprise. Being called out as an initiator will be jarring at first. But once it has happened to enough people enough times, a new paradigm will emerge. It is imperative that leaders model non-defensiveness to establish tone. We would recommend tapping into cultural competence coaching if this strikes leaders and managers as particularly challenging.

External Organizational Support

The authors of this book are not merely theorists. We are career diversity, equity, and inclusion (DEI) practitioners. We both have developed, studied, tested, and optimized learning systems and technology to help our clients increase inclusion and accountability. Our companies include the following:

TMI PORTFOLIO OF COMPANIES
Coaching, training and workshops, DEI strategy, train-the-trainer, DEI metrics, keynotes

One of Dr. Jana's portfolio companies, TMI Consulting, offers various types of executive inclusion coaching, training, and workshops to facilitate the development and internalization of these skills. Their company can also facilitate and lead the development of long-term diversity, equity, and inclusion strategy for organizations.

Dr. Jana's other portfolio company, Loom Technologies, can help you calibrate your organizational culture and measure the extent to which behaviors like microaggressions and SAE or unconscious bias are operating in your company. Loom's flagship product, Loom The Culture Map®, helps organizations measure, map, and improve organizational culture using machine learning.

INQUEST CONSULTING
Strategy and structure, D&I training and experiences, digital learning and sustainment, keynotes

Dr. Baran is a senior partner at inQUEST Consulting, which provides a variety of diversity and inclusion (D&I) strategy and training experiences to sustain D&I learning, growth, and behavior change. Several of these products and services directly address SAE and improving workplace culture with improved feedback conversations. One training course, From Unconscious Bias to Conscious Inclusion, for example, helps leaders build inclusive practices that not only increase inclusion broadly but can also specifically help leaders model productive SAE conversations.

In addition, Dr. Baran has developed an interactive digital learning path with activities that help people think through different SAE scenarios and explore different reactions, practicing more productive conversations. This digital "practice" that individuals can do on their own helps people explore the complexity of understanding and speaking up about SAE using videos of real people and scenarios based on real examples, such as those in this book.

One paradigm shift we are seeing with increasing frequency is that leadership is interested in sustainable, fully embedded diversity, equity, and inclusion. Some organizations seem less keen on stand-alone DEI initiatives. Embedding this SAE accountability system is precisely the type of approach that encourages and advances the DEI conversation at every level of an organization without a whole subset of committees, councils, and resource groups. We are not saying there is no place for these structures. They each have their purpose within specific strategies. But the bottom line is that we have slowly eroded our ability to engage in civil discourse about any conceivable topic. The United States, in particular, has arguably never enjoyed the luxury of authentic, honest, inclusive discourse about our most pernicious social issues. Embedding this structure and the supporting skills that strengthen it can take your organization a long way toward being able to internally manage even the most challenging subject matter. Our suite of companies, services, and products is available to support organizations of any size, industry, or location.

A Note for Diversity, Equity, and Inclusion Facilitators

If you, like the authors, are in the privileged position to facilitate or train groups of people around sensitive topics related to identity, you have surely encountered SAE in the context of group discussions. And you have surely had a lot of practice developing personal strategies that are like the SAE accountability system. Facilitators know that part of their responsibility is to keep individuals in the group safe from psychological harm. Creating psychological safety is an important characteristic of good facilitation. So when SAE happen, they are usually prepared. Coauthor Jana writes:

> A white, female, anti-racist facilitator in Virginia was leading a cross-cultural dialogue for a local nonprofit. One of the participants had notified her in advance that he was going to be late to the session because he was a Confederate reenactor and had an event that ended just before the racial healing session. By

the time he arrived, the discussion had already begun. In the moments after he sat down, the African American man whom the Confederate reenactor sat next to made a comment about Confederate sympathizers and how problematic he thought they were. The facilitator was the only person in the room, besides the man himself, who knew where he had been, and therefore, she knew that he had likely been offended by the statement.

She could have let sleeping dogs lie. She could have let him fend for himself. After all, no one else knew where the man had been, so he could have hidden in plain sight and possibly kept his offense to himself. The facilitator did not make that choice. Her duty of care to the group compelled her to speak up in service of racial healing for the group and protection of individual well-being. After the Black man made the comment, she said something along the lines of, "Lucky for us, I believe we happen to have wisdom in the room that may help shed light on diverse perspectives." She opened the door for the white man to walk through if he was comfortable. She asked if he wanted to share why he was late, and he did.

The two men then proceeded to have an eye-opening conversation in which the reenactor explained that participating in those events connected him to his family, even if he didn't agree with everything they stood for. The two men connected on the importance of honoring family and genuinely expanded their rapport and camaraderie through openness and listening for understanding. That might not have been possible without the intentional, skilled facilitation and quick thinking that the facilitator offered in service of the group.

While it does take years of experience to develop the skills to handle some of the more challenging aspects of diversity facilitation, being prepared for SAE can help create psychological safety for participants at any stage of the facilitation journey. Psychological safety is a concept defined by Amy Edmondson as "a shared belief held by members of a team that the team is safe for interpersonal risk taking."[1] The most important first step in a training or an organization is understanding that subtle acts of exclusion are bound to happen, and then creating room for these and other mistakes. This will help people feel safe from psychological and retaliatory harm when they make a misstep.

Name the behaviors you want to avoid and reinforce, and then be accountable. Understand that there are degrees of harm and there is a difference between calling someone the N-word (a more overt, intentional act of aggression) and unwittingly using an exclusionary term. Some people will try to hide behind concepts like "unconscious bias" to cover up their overt bias. Use caution, discernment, and clear definitions to avoid confusion.

Most facilitators are familiar with the paradigm of establishing ground rules. This is a facilitation best practice. Include a mechanism for naming subtle acts of exclusion. Let the group know that when someone inadvertently initiates an SAE, the facilitator and participants will agree to name the action and address it in the moment. This will help people feel safe in the room and gives everyone permission to name the SAE when they occur. This way, no one needs to feel shocked or alarmed when an intervention takes place. Remember, people do not tend to commit SAE deliberately, so they will likely agree to the ground rules. Ensure that naming SAE becomes a standard part of your facilitation practice.

What's My Role/Responsibility in Addressing SAE Institutionally?

When organizations take on the work of reducing systemic barriers to inclusion, different levels of personnel have different responsibilities. Executive leadership typically initiates changes by supporting them and sanctioning them from the top of the organization. This is not universally the case, though. As coauthor Jana notes in their previous book *Erasing Institutional Bias*, an increasing number of organizations are experiencing the removal of systemic barriers instigated by a groundswell of grassroots efforts from individual contributors. Sometimes the individual contributors are dispersed across the organization; often change is championed by a single brave soul. Regardless of where you are positioned in the organization, everyone has a role. The inclusion of the SAE accountability system will be most successful if everyone is aware of and prepared to accept their role.

Executive Leadership

Failure to secure ample leadership buy-in is one of the reasons D&I efforts fail. Executive leadership needs to be fully aware of and on board with the idea of the SAE accountability system. They need to understand what SAE are, what is at stake if they are allowed to persist and fester, and how they need to respond when they initiate them or observe them. Leaders should understand that it is no longer acceptable for workplaces to allow SAE to go unaddressed. It is the organization's responsibility to address them because if SAE are not actively discouraged, then they are tacitly encouraged. This can lead to an unwelcoming environment of disrespect that fosters harassing behavior instead of belonging.

Leadership needs to be the first to learn the system of SAE accountability so they can model best practices and set the tone for the rest of the organization. People in leadership positions already know that they are under a microscope—always being watched and assessed by employees. Leaders need to practice holding each other accountable and model servant leadership by working to create a healthy culture where people can withstand gentle, informed guidance without losing their cool. Likewise, they need to model gently addressing SAE using the system with their direct reports and others as they begin to observe the unwanted behaviors.

Perhaps the hardest and most important leadership responsibility is to *praise* people for calling out subtle acts of exclusion. Yes, you read that correctly. People need to be *rewarded* and thanked for using the system. That is the single fastest way to embed the system into the organization. Behavioral psychologists tell us that we tend to get more of the behavior we pay attention to. Some might argue that we may get more SAE because this system also pays attention to them—and it will certainly feel that way in the beginning. People will start noticing SAE everywhere. But that is good. As the culture is keyed up to SAE, the unwanted behavior is vocally discouraged while the naming of SAE is encouraged. Everyone will want to be on the receiving end of praise, versus being the initiator, called out for unwanted behavior.

The adjustment period will require grace and gentle handling. This is where the leadership role of extending kindness and normalizing imperfection will be most critical. Remember the first organizational tenet: expect SAE to happen. Reinforce that message. Help people feel safe in knowing that SAE will happen and will be addressed.

And leaders . . . don't get defensive! Visualize your happy place—on the court, at the beach, playing with your adoring pet, your last vacation . . . whatever it takes. Just *do not lose your temper* when you are inevitably called out. Employees will test the system when they catch your subtle acts of exclusion. The occasional oppositional defiant person may invent an SAE just to test you, so you must be prepared to remain calm. It won't feel any different to you whether it was a real offense or a manufactured one, so be prepared. Intent and impact will never be aligned and you will have no way of knowing whether or how much anyone is triggered. This system is ultimately for the greater good and will create an environment where people can work out their concerns without having to turn to HR and external litigation. After the initial buzz, everything will settle into a culture of mutual concern, respect, and belonging. Embedding SAE accountability is a very big deal. Implemented well, it can lead to reduced turnover and increased productivity, engagement, and sense of belonging.

Middle Management

If mid-level managers are responding to an executive-level impera-tive to implement SAE accountability, it can feel heavy handed and unnecessarily burdensome to them. It may also seem warm and fuzzy or unnecessary. This is not something managers should do just because they are told they must. SAE accountability is some-thing every manager should be eager to implement because it helps address many of the day-to-day challenges they typically face.

Managers either directly or indirectly deal with the things that irk their employees every single day. Whether you are a manager who has to field untold numbers of complaints about teammates' behaviors, old grudges, gripes, and gossip, or you only witness the resulting lack of engagement, reduced productivity, absenteeism, and workplace tension, you know that the things people say and don't say wreak havoc on organizational culture.

With SAE accountability, we disempower the most pernicious parts of the rumor mill and other counterproductive systems by empowering people to voice their grievances in the moment. The shared nature of these moments allows everyone to learn from the situation and discourages further replication of the unwanted behavior. The system does tend to open up the organization for new or expanded courageous conversations about potentially challeng-ing topics. Again, this is a good thing in the long run. It will require an adjustment period, but one that we argue is well worth the invest-ment of time and energy.

The biggest challenge for mid-level managers may be the emo-tional labor, emotional intelligence, and cultural fluency required to navigate these conversations well. Managers need not be experts in all things diversity, equity, and inclusion, but the more cultural competency managers can access, the easier these discussions tend to be. Unlike cognitive intelligence, emotional intelligence can be improved. The bottom line is that there are fewer surprises when one is knowledgeable about the types of things SAE tend to be about. Reading the rest of this book, then, is one way to help managers increase their access to cultural understanding and manage the emotional labor necessary to navigate these discussions across any number of demographic divides.

Managers have an outsized impact on the culture of most organizations. The frustrating thing for managers is that they are often blamed for things that are out of their control and in the hands of executive leadership. At the same time, employees don't tend to leave the company or quit the executive leadership. People leave their bosses. It can feel like a catch-22 for managers who want to instigate changes and have more responsibility but can't.

Implementing an SAE accountability system is something that can be done officially as a top-down imperative, or managers can implement it within their teams to improve communication and functioning. Managers can also advocate for this by pushing the idea up to executive leadership proactively rather than waiting for it to roll downward. Managers seeking to demonstrate their personal commitment to diversity, equity, and inclusion can leverage this system as a tool to help their teams, the organization, etc. SAE accountability needs champions to work well. The more champions the better. The good news is that you don't have to be perfect. You don't have to be representative of any particular demographic. In fact, contrary to some perspectives on DEI work, this would be a great system for white, cisgendered men to champion if they want to take it on earnestly. The system is designed to inform and improve interpersonal relations. So if you are willing to seek out learning and growth and cultivate a sense of belonging on your team, you are a shoo-in regardless of race, gender identity, age, etc.

Individual Contributors

Being an individual contributor (IC) can sometimes feel disempowering when it comes to defining your role in a larger initiative. This can be the case with DEI work as well. The authors of this book feel that individual contributors have among the most important roles in DEI work and particularly with SAE accountability. From a DEI perspective and an organizational development perspective, there is no business without individual contributors. ICs are the people who make everything possible. Schools can't educate without teachers. Goods and service providers can't sell without salespeople. Few companies of any size can even function without administrative support. Whether they are cleaning the building, building the widgets, coding the tech, managing the calendars, or designing the newsletter, individual contributors are the amazing men, women, and gender nonconforming folks who make business possible. For profit, nonprofit, government—it doesn't matter what sector or industry—organizations cannot function without the good people who wake up every day and keep choosing to come back and serve the mission.

We hope that managers and executive leadership never lose sight of this fact. If you are lucky enough to be an IC with leadership that has decided to take on SAE accountability—awesome! Learn the system. Practice it. Give managers and leadership feedback on what works and what doesn't. They need to hear from you and they need you to be brave and try it out. Be honest about the results and don't give up. Ask for support and keep trying. The result will be a workplace that doesn't suck, a place you will be excited to go to on Monday mornings. A place where people still slip up, but where you can stand in dignity and politely seek the respect that you and your colleagues (and everyone else on earth) deserve.

Work should not be a place where we are subtly injured on a regular basis until we have retreated into little cocoons of isolation and misery. Your employer wants your very best energy fully engaged in the workplace. It is perfectly acceptable to ask for SAE to be addressed in support of your bringing your best to work. It feels good to contribute to a workplace that sees you, hears your needs and concerns, and stands up for you when you are insulted.

Leadership wants you to feel as if you belong no matter who you are and where you come from. Even if they don't use that kind of language yet, that is part of the result of this work. It gives people voice, agency, and a sense of belonging that ultimately helps organizations thrive by nurturing a healthy, respectful environment where people feel welcomed. So your job is to take it on wholeheartedly.

Resist the urge to abuse the privilege and weaponize SAE accountability. This is not a tool to bludgeon that manager who ticked you off two weeks ago. Start with a clean slate. Give people time to learn what SAE are and how the accountability system works. Be gentle. Be kind. People can tell when you are just being a jerk. Seriously, humans are animals and we can smell cruel intentions. Move in a spirit of education and grace. Be forgiving. We promise you, one day it will be you who is identified as the initiator and you will wish for the same grace and kindness. Remember that people in organizations have obnoxiously long memories and if you behave irresponsibly with your new superpower, it will come back to bite you. As coauthor Jana tells all their clients at TMI, use your superpowers for good!

If your leadership has not approved the implementation of an SAE accountability system, then you may need to be the champion. As we have mentioned before, an increasing number of clients are approaching us because ICs have called for action on the DEI front. So educate yourself and advocate for this system. If you need help understanding how to instigate change as an IC in a system larger than yourself, read coauthor Jana's book *Erasing Institutional Bias: How to Create Systemic Change for Organizational Inclusion*.

5

Gender and Sexuality SAE

IN THE FOLLOWING FIVE CHAPTERS, we will play out some SAE scenarios that we have observed, researched, or been told about by people who have experienced these situations. There are so many varied SAE that people experience along different dimensions of diversity that the examples included represent only a small fraction of what we might have written about. The identifying details, including names and some contexts, have been redacted or changed. But the subtle acts of exclusion are real. While we cannot describe the situations in their full complexity, we offer readers a sense of the events and feelings accompanying the SAE. In addition, we describe any accountability as it was experienced. If accountability was absent, we describe accountability alternatives as described in previous chapters. These "What could have been" scenarios are inherently hypothetical, and there are many factors at play in whether people speak up and how others react to them. But in this book, we lean into that complexity to explore options and hopefully move closer to fuller SAE accountability.

How We See Gender and Sexuality

Before jumping into SAE related to gender and sexuality, it's first important to clarify how we think about those topics, because there is a lot of confusion and conversation about them. For some of you this section will sound overly basic and obvious; feel free to skip ahead. But for others, there is a lot of confusion and we don't take for granted that everyone is on the same page.

Let's start with babies. When babies are born, they are assigned a biological sex. This is related to visible reproductive organs—a penis or a vagina. Most of the time, the sex assigned is as binary male or female. For some babies, however, it's not so clear. These babies are often called intersex. You may think that being born intersex is extremely rare, but some estimates place it at about the same as having red hair (approximately 1 to 2 percent of the population).[1] A percentage of those cases don't appear as clearly intersex until puberty, while others (approximately one in 2,000 babies born) show a mix of male and female genitalia right at birth. In those cases, many doctors pressure parents to choose a sex and perform surgery so that genitals match the assigned sex of the baby. This surgery is extremely controversial; many argue that it is unethical.

That's what people mean when they talk about "biological sex." "Gender" is related to the *ideas* that go along with that biological sex. What are men like? What are women like? Parents talk about how their boys "naturally" love to play with trucks while their girls just "naturally" gravitate toward playing make believe with dolls. While this book is not going to get into the debate about whether there are any biological differences like that between the sexes, we will say that research suggests many of these characteristics that people think are natural are in fact socialized by cultural expectations and interpersonal interactions from the earliest years.

Once people have a baby that has been assigned the sex of a girl, many parents not only dress her in pink and decorate her room differently, but they interact differently with her. They give her certain toys and not others. They talk to her in a gendered way. This starts from day one. And it infuses almost every aspect of the way people interact with that baby. By the time that child is a toddler, they have been treated dramatically differently from a boy baby by almost everyone around them.

Developing children are picking up on much more than we give them credit for—in the environment, in the interactions, and in the culture. Their brains are developing at a staggering rate—one to two million synaptic connections are being formed per second.[2] When that girl is a toddler and likes to play make believe with dolls and it looks "natural" to adults, it may actually be something that has been subtly, almost invisibly conditioned that appears natural. If our culture were to radically shift the way we raise children in this gendered way, gender itself would be expressed differently.

As these children grow, the majority feel that the ideas about gender surrounding them pretty much match how they feel about themselves. Of course, there is a range. Some boys seem to exemplify the stereotypic representations of "boyness"—they love sports, play rough, can't sit still, etc.—while others don't. But within that range, most feel that they were assigned the sex that matches how they feel about their gender identity. These people (who feel that their assigned sex matches their gender identity) can be called cisgender, or cis. Most people just think of them as "normal," a problematic construction because of the way it excludes everyone else as "not normal."

The people who do not feel that their gender identity matches the sex they were assigned at birth may consider themselves transgender (or trans) and may alter their outward gender expression to match the gender identity that they feel represents who they are. They may change their name and their gender pronoun to match this changed gender identity.

Other people, and the numbers of people in this group are continually increasing, may feel that they don't identify as strictly male or strictly female. They may then identify as gender nonconforming, gender fluid, or gender nonbinary. Coauthor Jana falls into this category. People who identify as nonbinary or nonconforming may also prefer to use a different pronoun to reflect their identity, which may be a gender neutral pronoun such as "they" and "them," as in Jana's case, or one of the less common pronouns like "ze."

Some people may believe that transgender or nonbinary people are something new and unique. However, anthropologists and other social scientists have documented cases of other cultures that have gender constructions that include options beyond just a binary male and female. We are strongly of the opinion that all people should be free to express their gender in any way that makes them feel like themselves as an individual and that all these various gender identifications and expressions should be not only equally valued, but considered equally normal.

So far, we have discussed biological sex and gender. Sexuality is about who people are attracted to sexually and romantically. People who identify as men and who are attracted to people who identify as women would be called "heterosexual" as would people who identify as women who are attracted to those who identify as men. People who identify as men who are attracted to others who identify as men would be called "homosexual" or "gay," and those who identify as women who are attracted to others who identify as women would also be called "homosexual" or "gay," or "lesbian."

Just as with gender, sexuality is not just binary. If it seems as if it is binary, that's because of the way our culture tells us what is normal or natural. In fact, many people may be attracted to people of any gender but may feel that they must choose only one because of societal expectations. Or people may choose to explicitly date anyone they want, and may call themselves "bisexual" or "pansexual." Of course, gender and sexuality are much more complicated than that, and the ways that people think about themselves and who they are attracted to are constantly evolving. For that reason, it's especially important to always be learning and listening to others who identify as different from you. These kinds of productive SAE conversations are perfect for that.

In this chapter we will discuss SAE that happen to women and other gender minorities, all of whom can be considered marginalized along the gender axis compared to cisgender men. And we will discuss SAE related to those who identify as other than heterosexual.

Notice the Dynamic: Practice Identifying Common SAE

Let's look at a few gender-based SAE and see whether you can identify the operating dynamic based on the chapter 1 framework of what the subtle act of exclusion is implicitly communicating. Recall the taxonomy from chapter 1:

- You are invisible.
- You are inadequate.
- You are not an individual.
- You don't belong.
- You are not normal.
- You are a curiosity.
- You are a threat.
- You are a burden.

Read each of the following situations and think about what is happening. How might each group or individual be feeling?

- Situation 1: People extend a hand to introduce themselves to the male in a mixed-gender group, assuming he's the person in charge.
    - What kind of SAE is happening?
    - How might the woman in charge be feeling?

- How might the assumed male leader be feeling?

- How might the informed bystanders be feeling?

- Situation 2: A man is given credit for an idea that a woman had already explained during a meeting.

  - What kind of SAE is taking place?

  - How might the woman be feeling?

  - How might the man be feeling?

  - How might the other meeting participants be feeling?

- Situation 3: Employees are overheard making broad gender generalizations or jokes in the workplace.

  - What kind of SAE is being described?

  - How might gender minorities feel if they overhear the jokes?

  - How might inclusion allies be feeling?

In the first situation, folks are assuming that the man is in charge based on a bias (unconscious or not) that men are generally leaders. In the second, people are elevating male status and authority, giving more weight to an idea when the man said it. And in the third scenario, people are minimizing gender by making light of it and reinforcing a binary, stereotypical gender culture.

The taxonomy can be applied as follows:

- Situation 1: Assuming the man is in charge implicitly communicates that the female leader is **inadequate** for leadership.

- Situation 2: Giving a man credit for a woman's previously stated idea renders her **invisible**.

- Situation 3: Making gender jokes and generalizations in the workplace makes the subjects feel they **don't belong**.

The interesting thing to note here is that in each of these three scenarios, there were observers. These SAE took place in the presence of people who experienced the dynamic alongside the subjects. If they speak up, they could become allies.

Subtle acts of exclusion are tricky. They are, by their very nature, easy to miss or ignore, especially if you are not the person being offended or excluded. At one point early in the book-writing process, it was suggested that we name this book *Death by a Thousand Cuts* because of the way that microaggressions tend to follow people and cause increasing harm over time. Upon further thought, we realized, however, that the expression itself could be considered a microaggression.

"Death by a thousand cuts" is the translation of a specific type of torture and execution previously used in China, Korea, and Vietnam. Using that expression casually to draw a metaphor for microaggressions, while viscerally poignant, is culturally insensitive. And therein lies the rub. We weren't trying to be insensitive, but that fact does not alter the reality that bandying about interesting cultural references can still have the effect (impact) of exclusion, even if subtle and unrecognized by most people.

Gender has long been the cause of a wide variety of explicit acts of exclusion, structural inequalities, unfair and gendered expectations, and subtle acts of exclusion. Subtle acts of exclusion related to gender happen so frequently that we struggled to narrow down the examples we wanted to discuss in this chapter. Examples of gender SAE are extremely common in workplaces but also in the home as women and gender minorities negotiate work with those who love them the most.

In the home, even among progressive and equality-minded men, gender expectations run deep and they may come to the surface even more so if a couple has children. In fact, a recent *New York Times* opinion article entitled "What 'Good' Dads Get Away With"[3] virally passed among moms who shared commiseration and stories of their "good" husbands/dads. Examples include cluelessness ("Oh, there's no school tomorrow?"), forgetfulness, or just not seeing certain tasks as important (folding laundry), and using being "more laid-back" as an excuse to not share household tasks equally.

Even when SAE are happening in the home, they affect women in the workplace too. As the extra burdens take a toll on women (physically, mentally, emotionally), they impact the ease with which women are able to devote time to their jobs and they make it so that many women temporarily leave their jobs or take part-time work to raise children, which then limits their advancement when they are ready to return full time. It's hard to neatly separate the domains. In the following examples, we focus on a few of the more common and illustrative SAE that happen to women and gender minorities in their workplaces. Some examples are provided with more detail, in story form, beginning with the following example.

EXAMPLE: Cutting women off during work meetings and not giving them credit for their ideas

It's your division leadership monthly meeting and you are discussing strategy for increasing future growth in the face of declining market share. Tanya shares her idea that perhaps increasing the diversity of the team and including different perspectives would increase creativity and innovation. She gets very little acknowledgment for this idea. A few more suggestions are made. Then Randall looks around the room and suggests that he notices a distinct lack of diverse perspectives, especially women, which could be one reason for the lack of innovation. Randall gets acknowledged widely for having an important thought, and a decision is made to look at pipeline initiatives for getting more diverse perspectives into senior management.

Does this example sound familiar to you? If you are a woman in the corporate world, it likely feels all too familiar. Countless anecdotal examples and even systematic research bears this out.[4] This is a clear example of an SAE that is communicating, "You are invisible." If this happens repeatedly to women in meetings, strategy sessions, team planning, and other work contexts, there are several consequences.

Women may become disengaged in the work because they feel as if their contributions and efforts are not being seen. This is a normal and common reaction when someone is excluded by being made to feel invisible. When that happens, the work itself suffers, as it does not have the benefit of the full engagement of all team members. Additionally, if this happens, women may end up leaving the job and seeking a workplace culture where they are not invisible and can make a meaningful contribution. Finally, it affects happiness and satisfaction. Everyone wants to be seen, valued, and heard at work, and when we are not, it takes a toll on our mental state. The SAE affect the individual, the work product, the work culture, and the organization's bottom line.

What could potentially be done if you see this happening in your workplace? This is a great example of a time when an ally can be especially effective. If the woman who was cut off or not given credit speaks up, she can be seen as selfishly trying to advance herself. But if someone else in the meeting points out how Tanya had already mentioned that, it gives Tanya credit in what might be a more comfortable way. Everyone in those meetings can look for opportunities to speak up about SAE like that. In addition, when people at an organization know that this is likely to happen, they can practice disrupting and preventing this kind of SAE from even happening in the first place. People can practice active listening, they can develop policies for equal speaking time for all, and they can improve inclusive leadership practices.

The following are a few more examples of workplace gender-based SAE.

1. The women feel obligated to clean up after office parties/functions whereas the men don't.

2. The women are expected to tidy up the office kitchen or serve coffee.

3. The woman in a meeting is asked to take notes.

4. A woman is told to do any of the previous in a professional setting when it is not expressly part of her assigned job duties.

Notice the similarities between the first and second statements. In the first statement, women feel a sense of obligation to perform a stereotypically domestic duty often relegated to women. In the second sentiment, the expectation is external—or someone else is imposing their bias onto the target. The first is a form of internalized oppression, when marginalized groups unknowingly accept or "buy in" to some of the stereotypical or negative messages propagated about them and act accordingly.[5]

The third statement is a more overt SAE because the idea is being expressed aloud, although still in question format. Sometimes it is easy to fall into the trap of believing that if we present a question, the respondent has a choice. We will say more on this later. The fourth statement is the least subtle of the four SAE.

So here we see four very similar SAE constructs that affect women and gender minorities in the workplace. You can see how they range from internalized microaggression to fully expressed imperatives. The following four constructs relate back to the four examples listed previously in the same order:

1. Internalized marginalization

2. Stereotyped expectation (systemic/societal)

3. Indirect SAE (false choice/benevolent bias)

4. Direct SAE (fully expressed—stated, depicted, written, etc.)

By now you may be thinking to yourself, "OK great. SAE are a thing. Now what?" Now we get to the fun part, or the hard part— depending on how you feel about personal development work. We happen to love it. We believe that in an increasingly diverse world with increased access to information and to visiting new places, we have an obligation to grow together and learn to embrace human-kind in a more complete and loving way. The authors of this book share the perspective of diversity practitioners and researchers, and as such, we are proponents of the introspective work required to be an ally and evolve into embracing inclusive behaviors that build community. All work related to diversity, equity, and inclusion begins with oneself. You must take on the task of understanding the role you play in perpetuating bias.

Consider Workplace Boundaries

Some SAE happen because people take their curiosity, concern, or nosiness a little too far. In the workplace context, some things are not your nor the company's business. Read the following three scenarios then consider the follow-up questions.

- ▸ Situation 1: An employee makes statements implying that a mother isn't as committed to work because she has family obligations.
    - ▸ Are her family obligations any of the employee's concern?
    - ▸ Has she expressed an inability or lack of desire to complete her work obligations?
- ▸ Situation 2: A vendor says, "The women here are doing an amazing job, considering all they have to balance with the family too."
    - ▸ Again, are their family obligations any of the vendor's concern?
    - ▸ Is the second part of that statement necessary?
    - ▸ Would the same thing be said of a man?

- Situation 3: During an interview or when considering a promotion, a manager asks subtly probing questions to ascertain if a woman is interested in having children.

  - Is it legal to ask about parental status during an interview?

  - What is the connection between having children and the ability to perform the new position?

Here again is the taxonomy:

- You are invisible.

- You are inadequate.

- You are not an individual.

- You don't belong.

- You are not normal.

- You are a curiosity.

- You are a threat.

- You are a burden.

Now apply the taxonomy:

- Situation 1: Implying that a mother isn't committed to her work is an **inadequacy subtle act of exclusion**.

- Situation 2: Praising women for doing their job while having families is a **normalcy subtle act of exclusion**.

- Situation 3: Inserting a woman's family planning into the workplace implies her fertility is a **threat**.

Workplace boundaries become very important when it comes to gender because of sex discrimination. If a woman's desire to procreate gets in the way of a potential hire or promotion due to the possibility of maternity leave, that can be construed as sex discrimination.

Hot-Button Topics

Sometimes there is an uptick in SAE around hot-button topics as a society grapples with new ideas, or ideas that can no longer be relegated to the fringes. The conversation about gender pronouns and gender identity, for instance, has gained traction in some parts of the world. The United States, in particular, is starting to experience changes in the way people approach gender identity and its acceptance into the mainstream lexicon and culture. As far back as humanity has recorded social identities and expressions, people have chosen many different ways to express themselves. What is deemed acceptable or "normal" by any given society has always been a moving target.

Cultures associate certain behaviors, status, careers, attitudes, clothing, names, roles, and more with one gender or another. Many people have a low tolerance for or understanding of ambiguity, nonconformity, and fluidity. Interestingly, these constructs can be abstracted and applied to any manner of situations and be equally unsettling to people. So it stands to reason that when you place the concept of gender in front of the terms ambiguity, nonconformity, and fluidity, some people react with a range of emotions, from mild confusion to open anger.

Unfortunately, gender nonconformity creates cognitive dissonance for some people, which makes it a hot-button topic. Navigating any dialogue where a hot-button issue is present can be doubly daunting. This issue and how to address it is covered in coauthor Jana's first book, *Overcoming Bias: Building Authentic Relationships across Differences*. Here are a few more examples of gender-based subtle acts of exclusion.

- Situation 1: Someone calls a woman bossy.
    - Would they use the word "bossy" to describe a man?
    - Are the same behaviors being rewarded in men?

- Situation 2: A person assumes gender identity or cisplains someone else's nonconforming identity to them.

  - Is it appropriate to tell other people who they are or how they should identify?

  - What does assuming gender identity accomplish?

  - Do we need to know a person's gender identity?

- Situation 3: You make a big deal out of getting someone's gender pronoun wrong and apologizing profusely, thereby putting the burden on the offended person to make you feel better.

  - Are you trying to make the other person feel normal and accepted or are you looking for credit for trying?

  - Should that offended person have to be taking care of you and your emotions or should you be taking care to make them feel comfortable?

- Situation 4: A woman balks at a person's use of the pronoun "they" because "it just doesn't make sense grammatically."

  - Did this woman look up whether it is grammatically correct?

  - Does this woman think that people who prefer the pronoun "they" haven't thought a *lot* about this already?

  - Is this woman's inconvenience at using a pronoun in a new way greater than the other person's need to be identified properly?

- Situation 5: A Christian refuses to call a transgender person by their preferred pronoun for any reason.

  - Is that person's faith strong enough that they can treat the transgender person how they want to be treated without feeling threatened?

  - What does it really cost you to treat people kindly as they would like to be treated?

EXAMPLE: "I wish I was a lesbian."

Anna Dorn, a writer from Los Angeles, wrote on her blog a post called "Girl, no you don't" about straight women telling her, "I wish I was a lesbian."[6] She says every time it happens, she wants to light herself on fire. And while she doesn't talk about it as a microaggression, this most certainly is an SAE that the authors have heard in various forms from people with nonnormative sexualities. Some have told the authors that people tell them, "I *wish* I was gay. It would be so much easier just dating guys since all we want is sex," or "I *wish* I was bisexual—you have so much of a bigger pool to choose from!" Most likely, people who say these things to gay and bisexual people are not meaning to exclude, but rather quite the opposite. They are likely the people trying to explicitly demonstrate that they are so comfortable with the other person's sexuality that they would even embrace it if they were that way too.

While we don't want to dismiss that there may be nice things about being gay or bisexual, the fact that people can so flippantly exclaim that it must be easier without recognizing how it is much more difficult to be out of the "norm" is definitely an SAE that communicates, "You (and your struggles) are invisible." It is clearly not easier to be considered not normal—to have to go through growing up and feeling as if something is wrong with you. Suicide rates alone will tell you there is nothing easier about this—they are about five times higher for LGBTQIA young people.[7] LGBTQIA youth also have higher rates of depression and substance abuse and experience higher rates of aggression and violence.

Although things are better now in many ways than they were in the past, they aren't better for everyone. Put SAE aside for one moment and consider the reality for trans people. Trans people are exponentially more likely than cisgendered people to be overtly harassed, physically attacked, and even killed for "looking gay" and being the beautiful people they are. The brilliant performance artist and thought leader Alok Vaid-Menon explains that our trans brothers and sisters literally put their bodies on the line every day in service of LGBTQIA rights and says, "We are the reason the LGBTQIA movement is gaining momentum; because we are visible, people know you exist."[8] We have no way of knowing whether people we know have experienced this violence, this harassment, this depression, this trauma, so to assume that it's so "easy" is an SAE of invisibility that needs to be understood.

EXAMPLE: "What does your husband do?"

Kate married her partner Crista two years ago. They debated which finger to use for their wedding rings. Should they wear them on the left hand, as traditional heterosexual couples do, or should they use the right hand to signify something else, because they are a lesbian couple? Or should they use a different finger entirely? Kate works in a large corporation, and in the end, she figured she could blend in a little more by wearing the ring on the left hand. Two years later, she is astounded by how many people notice her ring and draw conclusions from it. She has become exasperated that almost without fail, heterosexual people assume that she is married to a man. They may ask her, "What does your husband do?" or they might invite her to a work function and ask if she is going to bring her husband.

She does speak up about this subtle act of exclusion. She doesn't make a huge deal about it, but if it's someone she works with or meets outside work, she does tell them that her partner is a woman. She has noticed a few things from doing this many times. First, people are very apologetic after she corrects them. For the most part she thinks that's a good thing. They seem to not only recognize that they made an incorrect assumption about her, but they also recognize that they probably make this assumption all the time. Second, she notices that those individuals that she corrects never make the same mistake again. They may initiate other SAE about her sexuality, but they never mistake her for heterosexual again. That gives her hope. But third, she also notices that it just keeps happening that people make this assumption, and she doesn't have a lot of hope that it will end anytime soon.

One of the reasons this kind of thing seems to keep happening is because culturally we still don't treat alternatives to heterosexuality as normal, even when we accept them. Of course, there are those who are explicitly discriminatory to LGBTQIA people. Some may base that on religion, others may base it on what they feel is "natural." But even the people who are explicitly accepting do not treat it as normal, and that is partly because it is baked right into our cultural "common sense" of how things work.

We divide bathrooms up into men's and women's; we start events with, "Ladies and gentlemen"; we joke with young boys about whether they have a girlfriend; we have children's stories that almost all completely portray heterosexual couples or so explicitly advocate celebrating non-heterosexual sexualities that the subtle message is still, "This is not normal." There are rare exceptions to this. Coauthor Baran recalls one children's book called *Uncle Bobby's Wedding* by Sarah S. Brannen in which a man marrying a man is treated as completely normal and not even the focus of the story. The focus of the story is on the man's relationship with his niece, who is worried that she will lose him if he gets married.[9]

Books like that aside, the overwhelming mass of messages that people of all ages receive is that gender binary heterosexuality is what is normal. There is little chance that a child growing up in this culture would implicitly think any different, even if they explicitly get a good number of messages celebrating LGBTQIA equality. What would it take to really treat all these gender minorities and sexualities as normal? It would just take changing the way we talk. If we are talking to a young man, it would be asking him if he has a crush on anyone rather than asking him if he has a girlfriend (or not asking the question at all because it's a little odd). It would take seeing someone's wedding ring and asking them if they want to bring their spouse or partner to an event and then listening for them to tell us who they are married to. It's both a lot and a little to ask. But it's something we must do if we are going to avoid committing these SAE that communicate to people that they are not normal.

6

Race and Ethnicity SAE

BEFORE DIVING INTO the many examples of subtle acts of exclusion based on ideas of race and ethnicity, we thought it was important to step way back and discuss how race and ethnicity became ideas that influence how we treat other people in the first place. As the cultural anthropologist coauthor, Baran regularly finds himself answering questions about what people often refer to as the "social construction of race." Typically, those conversations go something like this.

New friend: *So what do you do for a living?*

Baran: *I am a cultural anthropologist by training with some study in cognitive psychology too, and now I work with organizations to support their diversity and inclusion efforts.*

New friend: *How interesting. You know what I think? I think we're really all part of one race, the human race, and all the labels are just made up and people shouldn't be treated differently because of their skin color.*

Baran: *Yes, I'm with you on that.*

New friend: *So we've really got to stop focusing on race and stop talking about it and then it will get better.*

Baran: *Noooooooo!*

Anthropologists are very specific in what they mean when they say that race is a historical, cultural construction. It's a long story with a ton of research and a lot of small variations and minor disputes. But for the broad strokes, there is agreement. In a nutshell, they mean something like the following.

Genetic differences between people are very small, and they are largely surface differences. Modern Homo sapiens evolved in Africa and began spreading out across the globe a couple hundred thousand years ago. As they migrated into Europe, Asia, Australia, and finally the Americas, they evolved physical differences in response to environmental pressures, the most critical of which was the sun. Having melanin in one's skin, for example, was advantageous in some areas and disadvantageous in other areas. In fact, if you looked at the average skin color across the globe before long-range sea travel began in the 1400s, you would see a gradual range from darker around the equator to lighter as you got closer to the colder climates with less sun.

During that time, if you were to take a walking trip from Central Africa where average skin color was the darkest up to the northernmost areas of Europe and Asia where skin color was the lightest, you would find continuous variation along the whole way. There would never be a time when you would think to yourself, "That was one racial group over there and here is a clearly different racial group." And that would be true for all the different physical features that one might associate with race—skin color, nose shape, eye shape, body type, hair texture, hair color, etc. All the physical features come in spectrums of difference and they don't correlate neatly together. All of this is to say that racial groupings are more of an idea about difference than a description of actual biological difference.

Those ideas about difference developed historically, especially in the early years of the United States of America. As the country grappled with ideals about equality of people with the reality of economic systems built on slave labor, politicians suggested that perhaps all people were not actually biologically equal. Subsequently, anthropologists of the early 1900s began to study these biological differences between supposed racial groups, and lo and behold, they did "find" that there were biological differences. They developed typologies and hierarchies of the races. But it turns out that this was junk science and researchers have gone back to find flaws in the data and analyses of these scientists.[1] The bottom line is that racial constructs originated with racist ideas created to differentiate Black people from white people to justify the enslavement of Africans. Whiteness would not exist without Blackness. And much of the racial animosity that still plagues society is based entirely on lies and the delusion of white supremacy.

Nonetheless, our developing brains are quick to latch onto these purported racial groups and to naturalize them, to basically think like those race scientists of the 1900s. People tend to think about the world as divided into these natural racial groups that are bounded and biological and that carry all sorts of associations about value, potential, and characteristics. People don't think like this on purpose, but they often do think like this unconsciously. That kind of thinking continues over time precisely because we don't recognize and talk explicitly about the way that it gets perpetuated over time and the way that it creates (along with structural inequality) real consequences for people of color—disparities in wealth, housing, education, criminal justice, and health.

And it's that kind of group thinking that feeds SAE about race. If you take the example of calling a Black man articulate, for example, it's the background of thinking that all Black people share the trait of not being well spoken that allows the SAE to happen. And as such, we think it's important to point out these misconceptions about race and to build a deeper understanding that can help clarify what SAE are, why they are so important to address, and what we can do about them. That will be made clear in the following examples.

EXAMPLE: Clutching purse, locking car, crossing the street, etc. when seeing a Black man

This SAE is described as incredibly common by Black men. It is clearly an SAE that communicates, "You are a threat." Black men are seen as such a threat, in fact, that studies show that people even think they are physically larger than they actually are.[2] Black men who happen to be tall and muscular report going through life noticing this kind of SAE constantly—during leisure activities, running errands, and in their work. One Black man described going to a work meeting in a large downtown city, wearing a nice suit and tie, and noticing in the elevator mirror a woman clutching her purse tight as soon as he entered the elevator. As can be seen, this is predicated on the way that people unconsciously think there is something dangerous about *all*, not just individual, Black men. It doesn't matter how you look, what you are wearing, or who you are as an individual. You are perceived a certain way because of the way you are categorized and the associations that people have with that category. While this SAE likely occurs more with Black men, it also occurs with Black women and gender minorities.

The authors have heard people justifying this behavior as having some basis in reality. They may say something like, "Well, there's some truth to generalizations. If I cross the street because I'm afraid of someone walking toward me, that just makes sense. I have to be careful." We certainly think that people should be careful, and we emphatically agree that occasionally people have a gut feeling that a situation might be dangerous, and they should respect that intuition. However, we want to use research to push back against the idea that in the case of race, the bias that people have is reflecting some sort of reality. As previously mentioned, people's fears about Black men lead them to misperceive Black men as taller, heavier, more muscular, and more dangerous than they actually are. It is because of these conscious and unconscious biases as well as general unfamiliarity that people read Black people as a threat. And it is because of these *mis*perceptions that we see a recent spike in people calling the police against Black people doing very normal things like napping in their school lounge, using a public pool, entering their own homes, and grilling in the park.

Race versus Ethnicity

In this chapter, we present SAE related to both race and ethnicity, though there are easily enough examples that each could have had its own chapter (or own book!). Before getting to more examples, we want to explain how we are thinking about race compared to ethnicity.

Many people have an understanding that race is about biological differences and ethnicity is about heritage and culture rather than biology. Race deals with differences that are Black, white, Asian, Indigenous, etc. Ethnicity deals with differences within those categories. Within the category of white, people can consider themselves Italian, Irish, English, or Portuguese, for example. Within the category of Black, people can consider themselves African American, Jamaican, Haitian, etc.

However, those distinctions between race and ethnicity are not so clear cut in human minds. Put yourself in the shoes of a young child again, between birth and age three. As mentioned in the previous chapter, their brains are growing at an astounding rate, making between one and two million synaptic connections per second! Their brains are physically being built at this young age and beyond. As their brains develop, they are ready to learn specific kinds of information at distinct times. For example, for the most part, children's brains are ready to start learning how to understand language and to speak or sign at a particular time in their development. It happens very early, even though it's incredibly complex, because their brains are prepared to do that. And we don't need to teach them how to communicate in this way, we just communicate with them and they do it effortlessly. Of course, teaching children to read and write is quite different, as our brains did not evolve for that. But with communication, a child's brain actively picks out cues from the environment and constructs the knowledge structures based on what they encounter.

In a somewhat similar way, a child's brain is likely predisposed to pick out clues from the environment in terms of what groups exist in the cultural/social world that they are going to inhabit. Young children may not even appear to be paying attention when they overhear a parent saying something like, "Yeah, I'm excited that he's going to have a Black preschool teacher." The parent assumes the child is not even listening, but the child has learned a lot about the world from that one simple utterance. They learn that (1) there is a category of people called Black; (2) the other times my parent said the word "teacher," there wasn't a qualifier like Black in front of it, so it's marked in some critical way; and (3) my parent is excited about it, so it's important. The child then forms a cognitive placeholder and goes about subconsciously filling in more information about that category—who fits into the category and what characteristics and potentials are associated with that category.

As the child develops, they hear many categories of people like this—Black, white, and Asian, but also Hispanic, Jewish, Chinese, Muslim, Russian, etc. To a developing child, these categories often become what psychologists call "essentialized." That is, the child subconsciously thinks of these categories as real, bounded, natural things in the world that have real implications and associations. They don't learn the specific associations usually from explicit parental teaching—they learn from the subtle messages all around us in society—from the news, movies, and TV shows; from what adults say; and even from subtle behaviors they witness in everyday interactions (locking car doors in certain neighborhoods or when certain people pass, for example).

From this perspective, there is little difference between the way a child, and later an adult, differentiates cognitively between a category typically conceptualized as racial, such as Black or white, and one typically conceptualized as ethnic, such as Hispanic or Muslim. They are all cognized as natural groups of people, and our minds fill in assumptions and unconscious biases about them that then feed into subtle acts of exclusion. In fact, several years ago coauthor Baran conducted a small study going around to various locations on the street and asking people a series of interview questions. The first question was always, "What race do you consider yourself?" He interviewed 155 people like this and heard 71 different responses! People answered that question in terms of race, but also ethnicity, nationality, and even religion. We tend to think that it's clear what the difference is between these domains when we write out formal definitions, but it's not so clear cut in our minds.

EXAMPLE: "Where are you really from?"

Camile considers herself mixed race, with a mother who is Chinese American and a father who is African American. As she describes it, she is hard to label. And she is often approached by people who ask her, "Where are you from?" or sometimes "What are you?" She knows that they are asking about her race or her ethnicity because they can't easily assign her to a category. And she knows that most of the time, their intent is not bad. However, she has been asked this question so many times that she cannot always suppress her frustration. She replies, "San Antonio, Texas." She knows what's coming next. "Yeah, but where are you really from?"

In this example, people asking Camile where she is from are thinking that they are engaging her and that they are showing interest in who she is and what her background might be. But this SAE is communicating to her, "You are a curiosity," "You are not normal," and "You don't belong." The fact that it happens so often just reinforces those messages again and again, preventing her from feeling included because her racial identity always seems to be so top of mind for people she meets and interacts with. Additionally, the assumption really seems to be that she is not from the United States of America, that she is somehow less American because of the way she looks, even though she was born in Texas.

In fact, there is research showing that white Americans judge Asian Americans to be less American than white Americans, even when told that they were born in the United States![3] The question "Where are you from?" and the judgment that some people are perceived as less American does not only happen to Asian Americans, but to many people of color and especially those who are mixed race or deemed to look racially ambiguous. They are especially "curiosities" because they defy the simple, bounded categories that people have in their heads.

What could Camile say when people ask her this question? What could people who overhear the exchange say? Typically, when this happens, nothing productive gets said. Camile is incredibly frustrated but begrudgingly explains that her mom is Chinese American and her dad is African American and then forces a smile when her questioner says, "Oh, how interesting! I thought maybe you were Pacific Islander or something like that."

This situation could go much more productively when following the guidelines outlined in chapter 3. Let's imagine that in that situation, Camile stops her questioner right away. He says, "Where are you from?" and she replies, "Hold up. I know you're not meaning anything bad by that question, but it's something that I get asked a lot, like almost every day. That exact question.

It makes me feel bad, like you're implying that I don't belong here. It would be nice to get to know more about each other, but this isn't the right context for that." The coworker in this situation has practiced what to do when this happens. Instead of defending his intention of just trying to ask her a question, he says, "OK, I'm hearing you. That question seemed innocent to me, but you hear it again and again and it makes you feel bad. I'm sorry about that. I'd love to sit together at lunch some day and learn more about you in a way that feels better."

At this point, we want to remind you that these are not scripts that need to be memorized. And you don't have to say the perfect thing every time. The most important points are that someone says something, not letting this SAE slide, and that the person who said the SAE has practiced not being defensive but really hearing the comment and taking it in. Another variation may be that a coworker overhears the question "Where are you from?" being asked of Camile. This coworker comes over and says, "Hold up. I'm not exactly sure why, but I did hear something about how that question can sometimes make people feel bad. Camile, are you OK with that?" Camile may say, "Thanks for saying something. I don't feel like talking about it now actually; I'm late for a meeting." The questioner might then say, "I don't really know what's wrong about that, but I'd like to learn more. Could we come back and discuss this tomorrow?" They used the technique of cooling off for more productive discussions. And they would make sure to not just let it go, but to come back to it when they were all ready to discuss.

EXAMPLE: Mistreating someone's name (not remembering, not trying to get it right, or even laughing at it)

This SAE was on full display during the broadcast of the Oscars in 2017 as Jimmy Kimmel subtly implied that only white sounding names are "normal." First, he attempted to joke about the name of Mahershala Ali's daughter (Bari Najma), asking, "You can't name her Amy?" Then when a group of unsuspecting tourists entered the awards show, Kimmel asked a woman for her name. She answered, "Ulery" (apologies if we're misspelling the name). Kimmel made an expression of shock and asked, "What?" Obviously accustomed to this reaction, Ulery explained, "It rhymes with jewelry." Kimmel said, "Wow, that's some name." He then asked the man she was walking with for his name. He replied, "My name's Patrick," to which Kimmel responded, "See, that's a name." The implicit message is that white, Western sounding names are legitimate while others are not. In the broadcast, you can see Ulery laughing, and yet, the idea that her name is an odd curiosity probably lost its humor a long time ago. Many, in fact, pointed out Kimmel's problematic jokes about names on Twitter afterward.

Depending on the specific way that a name is mistreated, these SAE could be communicating several implicit exclusion messages. When names are completely forgotten and people don't even try to pronounce them correctly, it communicates, "You are invisible." When people laugh at a name because it's not something they are familiar with, it communicates, "You are not normal." And when someone doesn't even try to remember a name, or even worse, substitutes a random association in place of the name ("Mr. Chang Wang" for an Asian name, as one author witnessed), it communicates, "You are not an individual."

Certainly we are not going to remember the name of everyone that we meet, especially when your job may require that you meet a lot of different people. And names that are unfamiliar may be even harder to remember or pronounce. It is fairly easy, however, to ask simple follow-ups, such as "Can you repeat that?" "How do I pronounce that?" or "How do I spell that?" to help get the name right. Those kinds of clarifying questions take an extra moment but they increase inclusion for the recipients.

When done genuinely, they express, "You are valued," and "You are an individual."

EXAMPLE: "I don't even see you as Black."

Janelle (Black) had recently joined the organization where Margo (white) had worked for a couple of years. They were both in the same department and at the same level. They talked a lot at work and even started to go to the deli across the street to get lunch together on Fridays. As they became closer, they would discuss events outside of work, including current events. During one of those discussions, Janelle said something like, "Maybe it's because I'm Black, but I see things like this," and gave her opinion. Margo, intending to show closeness and to demonstrate a lack of any prejudice, said, "I don't even think of you as Black." She wasn't prepared for the effect that this would have on Janelle.

Janelle was upset and said something right away. "But I am Black. And I actually want you to see me as I really am." Margo tried to backpedal, explaining that she just meant that she saw her as an individual and her friend. Janelle understood that but struggled to explain why it made her feel so uneasy when Margo said it.

Subtle acts of exclusion like this communicate, "You are invisible," but in a complicated way. In order to acknowledge someone's individuality, certain aspects of who they are get ignored. Additionally, Margo is subtly communicating, "Those stereotypes or associations that I have of Black people don't seem to be true with you, and so you don't seem Black to me." This is a common and fascinating mental trick that human minds play. They have cognitive categories and associated values, characteristics, etc. that are applied to groups in general. As people in those groups become known as individuals, our brains don't change the associations of the group, they just consider that person an anomaly from the group. In the case we've been discussing, Margo's brain doesn't change the category of Black to account for what she now knows about Janelle, but rather she considers Janelle an exception, set apart from the group stereotype.

This sort of thing happens frequently. Even people who have explicit biases against a group can be friends with individuals of that group, thinking they aren't real members of the group. It leads people to say various similar SAE like, "You don't act Black," or "Why do you sound white?" or "You're not a real Latina."

EXAMPLE: "You people"

Conversely, instead of singling out an individual from the group, other SAE may lump everyone in a group together: "You people," "Your people," "The Black community." People may expect you to speak for everyone in your marginalized group. When this happens, it is inherently otherizing. Referring to anyone or any group as "You(r) people" creates separation. It implies that we are fundamentally different from you in some meaningful way and also homogenous in some meaningful way. And yes, cultural norms, patterns, and tendencies may be real differentiators. That does not give anyone license to weaponize those distinctions.

We don't use the term "weaponize" lightly. But when someone accesses this language of separateness, the implication is rarely that the "other" is superior. One essentially elevates oneself to a superior status by using this language. And again, it's typically not an intentional choice to diminish the subject. Yet, by spotlighting their otherness, they are casting judgment that is not usually uplifting. This is precisely why we must think before we speak.

EXAMPLE: Touching a Black person's hair

Let's walk through how one common SAE could be addressed in the workplace. Jordan is an African American woman working in a large company. She is outgoing, warm, and kind with a large, diverse group of friends as coworkers. One day her team is working on a project together. Everyone is sitting around a conference table, looking at the projection of someone's laptop screen. Hannah is a white woman. She arrives a little late to the meeting, and as she arrives, she starts going around the table greeting everyone, giving little hugs to those she knows best. As she hugs Jordan, she pats her hair and says, "Wow, your hair is looking great today." Jordan's hair was looking great that day, but she considered that an SAE, communicating, "You're a curiosity." On this day, in that setting, Jordan didn't have the energy to say anything in the moment.

What if everyone in that room had been trained on the SAE accountability system? Then, when Jordan didn't feel like speaking up, Natalie, a white woman, might have been able to step up as an ally.

She could begin by first **pausing the action**. She might say, "Hold on, Hannah. Hold on, everyone. Sorry, I would like to address something that just happened." This is certainly risky, pausing a meeting to address something like this. And Natalie might not always feel comfortable doing it. But with everyone in the room having gone through the training, and with a high degree of trust on the team, she might feel as if this was a good learning opportunity.

She would quickly set some context and **assume good intent**. "Hannah, I know you are good friends with Jordan and would never do anything intentionally to hurt her."

She would then move to **explaining why the action was paused**. "This might not even be an SAE. I'm not sure. But I know I've always heard that it can be an SAE to touch Black women's hair. I know you were just complimenting her, but you also did touch it in the process. Jordan, do you want to say anything about this or would you rather not?" Jordan might say, "Yeah, I was just going to let this go, but I guess it did bother me. It happens so often, less these days but more when I was younger. It just makes me feel as if I'm being pet. And it makes me feel as if people must really think my hair is strange, rather than normal. And it sometimes messes up my hair, which I put a lot of work into looking good. I don't love it."

Hannah might feel embarrassed. She might even know that this is a thing that she is not supposed to do. But if she has practiced having the first thing out of her mouth be **acknowledging the discussion with gratitude**, she might say, "Natalie, I'm really glad you brought this up. I am embarrassed now but would have been much more embarrassed had I realized this later. I'm grateful for the opportunity for us to discuss this."

In her head, Hannah might desperately want Jordan to know about her intention, which was to compliment and to show how much she cares for her. But she has practiced **not being defensive, but curious and empathetic instead**. She would know not to clarify her intention, which would be defensive. She would have learned to think about the impact on Jordan and the room rather than her intention. And she would have practiced looking at the situation from Jordan's perspective. She asks a question, instead. "Have I done that before? Is there anything else I do that feels bad to you?"

At this point, Jordan might not be feeling like having the conversation continue at the expense of the work that they really need to accomplish at the meeting. She might say, "Let me think about that and get back to you. It's all good, I'm glad we had this conversation, but for now let's go back to figuring out how to move forward on this project."

The next day, Hannah would **follow through and follow up**. She might swing by Jordan's office first thing in the morning. "Jordan, do you have five minutes? I really wanted to apologize again to you and to let you know that I did some Googling of blog posts and have a better sense of all the issues involved with that one little gesture. Not so little after all. There's a lot of history and feelings there." Jordan might feel more understood and say something like, "It's really OK. It's great that we can grow like this and not have it derail our relationship." Hannah would also follow up with Natalie, the ally, when she sees her by the coffee machine. "Natalie, I wanted you to know I really did appreciate the way you spoke up about what happened yesterday. I was definitely embarrassed, but have already talked to Jordan this morning and feel better." Jordan might also reach out to Natalie later at lunch and say, "Thanks for speaking up yesterday. I might have just let it go because I don't have the energy to address all these subtle acts of exclusion. But I'm glad to not have to do it all on my own. It makes a difference."

Does this always go so smoothly? No, it does not! But it has a much better chance of going smoothly if everyone is familiar with the SAE accountability system. After the training, workshops, and scenario practicing, it really can be addressed in the moment like this. Instead of being an unacknowledged act of exclusion that would have cumulatively built up to make Jordan feel less included and less valued than she should feel, the moment can build inclusion and closeness with positive ripple effects across all those who were at that team meeting. The impact of one powerful discussion like this can be exponential. Others are less likely to do that same SAE, are more likely to speak up, and when they do speak up, they are more likely to do it in a productive way.

EXAMPLE: "No problemo"

Recently, coauthor Baran was watching a football game with some friends and family, and one of the guys was really hoping his team was going to get a field goal. It wasn't a very long one, and he said, "No problemo." This kind of playful way of adapting Spanish to different circumstances is incredibly common. The authors hear variations of it all the time. Baran remembers first thinking critically about this when he was teaching anthropology at the University of Michigan back in 2004 and had come across an article on what linguistic anthropologist Jane Hill calls "mock Spanish." It's the idea that non-Spanish speakers can attempt to be funny or clever by butchering Spanish phrases. They might say things like, "Exito only," or "No bueno." Examples abound, including things like "Hasta la vista, baby" from the *Terminator* movie and "Grassy-ass" seen on greeting cards instead of gracias.

Watching this football game, there were no native Spanish speakers around. As is often the case when these mock Spanish words are uttered, there was no one present of Hispanic or Latinx descent. Some may say, "What's the harm, then?" This example allows us to clearly explain why SAE are still a problem even when the subject of the SAE isn't present. The SAE still serve to communicate to all those present, in this case several family members including a whole bunch of children, that the subjects of the SAE aren't valued and respected. Spanish language, in this case, exists for the enjoyment and entertainment of dominant English speakers, even though incorrectly using English can have huge repercussions for non-native English speakers in public or at their jobs.

The recognition that SAE can happen in spaces where the subjects are not even present is critical. In the first place, it's where many SAE happen—when people are free to express themselves without filtering some of the things they might filter if others were present. Coauthor Baran, as a cisgender, heterosexual white man, notices many SAE based on race, ethnicity, gender, and sexuality when subjects are not present. And what he has come to realize is that people are so free in this way partly because they are never challenged about the SAE that they say in those situations.

This is exactly why it's so powerful when people speak up about these SAE even when the subjects are not present. That communicates the message that inclusion is important for all of us, all the time. The message is often received in a more impactful way because it cannot be simply dismissed as being sensitive about one's identity. On that day watching football, when Baran spoke up about the SAE, he could tell that it really affected the thinking of the initiator deeply and could see that he was thinking about it over the next few days. That's so exciting and promising, and it validates the idea that observers can become allies even when subjects are not around. And in fact, initiators can become allies when they learn from their own mistakes and speak up when they see those same SAE being committed.

We can see many folks protesting this idea of mock Spanish by citing the fact that tons of people in the country speak Spanish, even if it is not their native language. They might be thinking that we're suggesting that there shouldn't be any playfulness around Spanish words or phrases. That is not what we're saying, and in fact there are places where the two languages are inextricably mixed in the way people interact, sometimes in what is colloquially known by the portmanteau "Spanglish." However, in this case, people speak both languages (or speak one and are learning the other) and can playfully mix them around. This is not showing disrespect, dominance, or exclusion of the more marginalized language, so it is typically not considered an SAE. On the other hand, it is usually someone who does not speak Spanish committing the SAE because they are playing around with the *idea* of Spanish rather than the language itself.

EXAMPLE: "You don't speak Spanish?"

Karol's parents came to Connecticut from Puerto Rico before she was born. Her parents made frequent trips back to Puerto Rico with her to see friends and family, especially grandparents.

They made many efforts to make sure she spoke Spanish as they did. But Karol was going to school with people who for the most part spoke only English, and she wanted to fit in. As time went on, she became embarrassed by her Spanish when she spoke with people in Puerto Rico because they laughed at her accent or her inability to express certain things. This made it so that she really resisted Spanish, to the point where once she got to high school she really didn't consider herself a Spanish speaker.

When she went to college and began meeting lots of new people, they would often ask her questions about her heritage, and they assumed that she spoke Spanish. Sometimes other Hispanic people she met would just start talking to her in Spanish. And people in general were really surprised that she didn't speak Spanish. They would express that directly to her, as if to communicate, "You're not normal." In essence, they were communicating, "You're supposed to be a certain way because you look a certain way, and if you don't it's odd and you need to explain." It happened often and would cause her anxiety every time she met someone new. When she began working at a global company, people would often try to ask her questions about copy in Spanish or bring her onto teams discussing Latin America strategy. She sometimes thought that people were thinking she was lying about her inability to speak Spanish or that they considered this a real weakness.

EXAMPLE: "You're Korean? I was so close!"

Amy had recently started at a new company in the IT department. There were not many women in the department, but there were a decent amount of people that ethnically looked like her. She was ethnically Korean, and her parents had immigrated to the United States before she was born. During one monthly staff meeting, the administration ordered the food for the meeting from the local Thai restaurant. Everyone stood in line, got their food, and sat down for a few minutes of eating and small talk before the meeting began. Jason struck up a conversation with Amy about the food. "I've heard that the Thai food you get in Thailand is so much different from what you get here in the US. Is that true?" Amy was pretty used to these kinds of comments. People especially seemed eager to talk to her about a wide variety of Asian foods. And sure, her mom did cook some great Korean food, but any other food from Asia she had only experienced in restaurants just like everyone else.

"I don't know, I've never been to Thailand," Amy replied and kept eating. "Oh, I was sure you looked like you were from Thailand. Where are you from then?" Amy knew that Jason wouldn't rest until he had his answer, so she simply said, "I was born in Naperville, near Chicago. But my parents are originally from Seoul, South Korea." Jason's response was "You're Korean? I was so close!" As he then explained how much he loved kimchi, Amy couldn't wait for the meeting to start.

In this SAE, Jason is inadvertently communicating several things. First, he is communicating, "You don't belong," and "You're not normal," by assuming that Amy is somehow different or less American because of her look. Even when he hears she was born in Naperville, he still says, "You're Korean," assuming she is less American because of her heritage. Jason is also communicating, "You are not an individual," in the way that he makes assumptions about Amy and her life experiences simply by the way he reads her observable appearance and the way that he implies that he was "close" by guessing she was from Thailand.

Jason is also communicating, "You are a curiosity," in the way that he probes about background and attempts to bond with her over his surface understanding of Korean culture and food rather than asking questions about her and her experiences specifically. "Asian American" is an umbrella term that came into being in the 1960s. Most people who are identified as Asian American actually identify with more specific ethnic identities such as Chinese American, Korean American, Vietnamese American, etc. The US census even names these specific terms as categories under the race question. But what many have come to know is that people assume a great deal of commonality across these vastly different places and cultures, blurring differences and creating new stereotypes.

EXAMPLE: "Your accent is so cute."

Fatima's family immigrated to Queens, New York, from Pakistan when she was seven years old. She has been speaking English her whole life but does have a slight accent when she speaks. In Queens, there were so many different accents and languages around that her accent didn't really seem like a big deal to her. But as she moved into her role as a human relations associate at a large corporation in Pittsburgh, she found that there was a much more standard way of speaking and that people seemed to comment on her accent a lot. At the beginning, it felt OK when people would say, "I love your accent," or something similar because she also loved her accent. But it began to feel really patronizing and diminishing after a while, and even worse, it felt to her as if she was being overlooked for presentation opportunities. This SAE is communicating, "You are a curiosity," and also potentially, "You are inadequate," as it relates to Fatima's speaking ability.

Most of the time, Fatima held onto a forced polite smile when someone commented on her accent. But one time she snapped at a coworker from Sales named Caroline. They were chatting in the kitchen during bagel Wednesday about the quality of Pittsburgh bagels compared to the bagels from New York City. Caroline said, "Your accent is so cute. I love the way you say 'bagel.'" Fatima replied, "Yeah it is cute, much nicer than the Pittsburgh accent, which is terrible," and she left the room, leaving her bagel behind in the toaster.

Fatima was feeling flustered for the whole rest of the day. She felt angry and she also felt embarrassed and ashamed that she had snapped at Caroline. Near the end of the day, she felt as though she had calmed down enough to find Caroline and talk it through. But by then, Caroline had left for the day, and Fatima was left to worry about it and try to compose emails about it until late in the night. Fatima and Caroline hadn't been trained on the SAE accountability system. They both ended up feeling bad; they didn't get any closure; they didn't feel understood or included; and a lot of the burden to make things better fell on Fatima, even though she had been the one who experienced the SAE.

Let's walk through how this SAE could have been addressed using the SAE system. When Caroline made her comment, Fatima could have begun by first **pausing the action**. She could have said, "Hold on, Caroline. I would like to address something you just said."

She would make sure to quickly **assume good intent**. "I know you were just trying to compliment me. And to be honest, I think my accent is pretty adorable too."

Then she would **explain why the action was paused**. "But that being said, I am finding that people here comment a lot on my accent, and it makes me feel bad, as if I'm not normal, or a curiosity. And even more, I actually worry that it gets held against me sometimes."

Saying something like that would have a good chance of putting Caroline at ease. She might be able to hear what Fatima is saying pretty easily. Caroline would first **acknowledge the discussion with gratitude** and say, "Fatima, thank you for saying something." Then she would **replace defensiveness with curiosity and empathy**: "I can see how to me this is just one little conversation but you're having to deal with this all the time, and it's not just a little issue. I'm grateful that we got to discuss this and that I can be more careful with things like this."

Fatima might then feel heard and included. "Thanks for being such a good listener. I feel really heard. Now if you would just hear me also about how much better New York bagels are!" They laugh and move on with their day. Humans being as they are, Fatima and Caroline might both still think about the incident all day, but hopefully not in a distraught way, but more from a feeling of pride that they were able to handle this in a productive way where everyone felt valued.

The next day, Caroline could **follow up** with Fatima, even by writing her an email, saying, "Hi Fatima, I just want you to know that I thought more about what you said and I really see where you are coming from. I feel terrible that I made you feel bad, but I do feel good about how we handled the situation. Hope you have a great day!"

This small interaction could go quite differently, depending on whether Fatima and Caroline had practiced the SAE accountability system. But the ramifications are huge. Productivity for the day would decrease for both individuals when they aren't able to resolve the situation quickly. Inclusion goes down for both of them, and trust is eroded when the situation doesn't get resolved. On the other hand, with a simple resolution like the one described, time is not wasted, people feel good and included, a new stronger connection is made between colleagues in different departments, work morale increases, and then all these benefits ripple out. It's for that reason that this understanding and training are so critical for organizations these days.

7

Ability SAE

A GREAT MANY PEOPLE become instantaneously offended and defensive when the topic of privilege emerges. We want to take a moment to mention that privilege is real and not relegated to any single class, race, gender, or other demographic. We all have some degree of privilege, as indicated in coauthor Jana's TEDx Talk, "The Power of Privilege." Privilege, simply stated, is any advantage that an individual or a group has that eases their success, advancement, or path in life.

This chapter is about abilities and diverse ways that abilities manifest in humans. Different people are differently abled and that is an accessible way to help people understand privilege. If you are temporarily able-bodied, in good health, and able to move yourself from one building to the next without much of a struggle—you have privilege. If you do not have to consider and research the physical accessibility of each space before you travel—you have privilege. If your mind works smoothly, unhindered by past brain injury or stroke, unlikely to lose momentum because of depression, able to concentrate without difficulty, you have privilege. Ability is a unique, core dimension of diversity in that any of us can instantly lose these physical and mental privileges with zero notice.

Often when we think of differently abled people, or people living with disabilities, we think of someone who has managed a certain condition for some time. Perhaps it's a wheelchair, or blindness. But have you considered, at length, the people who are going along as able-bodied, and suddenly tragedy strikes and they lose a limb or part of their mental capacity? Even depression is an ability challenge, diagnosed or not. Depression, anxiety, and other cognitive and emotional mental health constraints are typically incurable. We can treat the symptoms, but we cannot erase the condition, thereby rendering them permanent disabilities. In the United States, people living with such conditions are federally protected by the Americans with Disabilities Act (ADA).

There is a wide range of disabilities, and the lived experiences of people with those disabilities often remain somewhat of a mystery to those who have the privilege of being able-bodied and neurotypical. A lot of the subtle acts of exclusion that happen to these folks happen because of a lack of closeness, of familiarity, of basic understanding. Hearing from people who are disabled themselves is critical to build that basic understanding. A simple way you could do that right now from wherever you are is to go to Twitter and search the hashtag #disabilitytwitter. Sometimes getting a glimpse into those conversations brings a new lens of understanding.

Coauthor Baran was recently attending a conference in Chicago called Disability:IN, focused on increasing employment opportunities for people with disabilities and inclusion for those same people once hired. In a session called "Disability Etiquette 101," people on a panel talked about even basic things like how to talk about people with disabilities. Some on the panel mentioned that many people prefer person-forward language like "person with a disability." They don't want to be defined by their disability. Other people said they prefer to be called "disabled person." To them, it is part of their identity, and they talked about how it links them to a community of people, to activists who have come before them fighting for their rights, to a culture. People talked about disliking words that made them feel "broken," such as "hearing impaired," and instead preferred simple descriptors like "deaf" or "hard of hearing," "blind" or "low sight." The key takeaway about language was that there is no one preference for everyone and so just asking people what they prefer is a good way to be inclusive.

Let's consider a few examples of subtle acts of exclusion that happen to people living with disabilities.

EXAMPLE: Using a microphone

Alexis was participating in a two-day work retreat, one of the main themes of which was diversity and inclusion. There were approximately fifty people at the retreat, which was taking place in a medium-sized conference room. The retreat had a facilitator who led the team through exercises and a lot of discussion. At the start of the retreat, the facilitator asked everyone to speak their comments into a handheld microphone that was being passed from person to person. Many people rolled their eyes when passed the microphone. Some said jokingly, "You know I'm plenty loud and do not need this thing!" before their comments. Others said things like, "Oh, I hate these things," and then maybe half used the microphone. Many just started speaking without even waiting for the microphone to be passed.

Alexis didn't have any trouble hearing people without a microphone. But she was sensitive to the fact that other people might. And in fact, she knew that one of the people in the group struggled to hear. Alexis was one of a handful of people who spoke up when someone started speaking without the microphone. They would say "mic" right when the person started speaking, to remind them to wait for it to be passed. It ended up happening so consistently that Alexis felt the need to speak up. At one point during the conversation, she raised her hand and said, "I know it can be awkward to use a microphone and that people aren't used to using it, aren't used to hearing their voices with it. But there may be people in here who don't hear as well as others, and that amplification can be really helpful to them so that they can fully participate in the meetings."

For the rest of the retreat, people were a little better about using the microphone. They explicitly understood what Alexis had said and they were actively trying to comply. And yet, they would still do subtle things like roll their eyes or pause and make a face at the microphone before speaking. A few even tried to make jokes about it like when someone took the mic and said, "First, I'd like to thank the Academy." People laughed. The CEO even made a face when he got passed the mic.

Throughout all of this, Alexis was really frustrated. She kept thinking of Marina, the person she knew had trouble hearing. She imagined Marina feeling bad every time someone made one of these jokes or gestures. Although people had overtly stopped saying they didn't want to use the mic, they couldn't stop from making the subtle acts of exclusion, implicitly communicating to Marina "You are not normal," and even "You are a burden." If you are someone like Alexis who sees what's happening and even speaks up once, what are you supposed to do if it keeps happening? You know the burden for speaking up shouldn't fall on Marina. But you also might worry that if you speak up again, you're going to come off as disruptive. We can imagine feeling pretty hopeless in this situation.

What if Alexis and her colleagues had practiced SAE accountability? What might have gone differently? In the first place, people would likely have listened more actively and empathetically when Alexis spoke up. They would have understood better that their eye rolling and jokes were communicating something implicitly—that "You are a burden" or that "You are not normal." And they would have really practiced following through with adjusting their behavior.

Even if someone continued making SAE, however, more observers would have spoken up to be allies, not just Alexis. This would have amplified the impact and taken some of the burden off that one person. In fact, one of the people speaking up may have been a senior leader, which would have carried even more weight. And finally, there would have been follow-up with Marina, making her feel included rather than excluded. Collectively, the room would have created an inclusive culture that doesn't let anything slide. And it wouldn't have been that hard to do.

EXAMPLE: "You're such an inspiration."

Jerrold works in a federal government agency, and part of his job is to spread awareness about accessibility issues in the workplace. He is a little person himself, and when he gives presentations about accessibility issues or when he participates on panels discussing those issues, he often weaves in personal reflection and stories. He enjoys spreading the word on these important topics. But one thing he doesn't enjoy about the public presentations are the inevitable SAE that come.

After one recent talk, someone came up and told him, "You're such an inspiration." It happens a lot. People gush about how inspired they are by what he has accomplished or that he is so brave for doing the work. He sees on social media what people have called "inspiration porn"—videos of people with no legs getting a black belt or people with Down syndrome making a shot in basketball. Charlie Swinbourne, in the *Guardian*,[1] for example, talks about how advertisements use inspiration porn and how it has happened personally to him, as people tell him he is brave for being deaf and working in media. He writes that this patronizes people, communicating that expectations are so low that the fact that people with disabilities can accomplish these things is surprising and inspiring because of their "abnormality." "These disabled people's achievements are not enough on their own—their value really lies in what they can make everyone else feel like doing."

Groups and hashtags have formed to combat some of this particularly subtle kind of exclusion based on ability. For example, #stopmakingitweird has a website that asks people to take a pledge:[2]

- ▸ I PLEDGE to treat people with disabilities just like anyone else.

- ▸ I PLEDGE to only use language that is respectful toward people with disabilities AND that I would use to describe anyone else.

- ▸ I PLEDGE to not engage in excessive celebration when a person with a disability completes an ordinary task or activity.

- ▸ I PLEDGE to not subscribe to, share, or aid in the proliferation of "inspiration porn." Inspiration porn is an image of a person with a disability, often a child, doing something completely ordinary—like playing, or talking, or running, or drawing a picture, or hitting a tennis ball—carrying a caption like "Your excuse is invalid" or "Before you quit, try."

Another hashtag, #AbledsAreWeird, facilitates people with disabilities sharing some of these subtle behaviors and getting support for the SAE that they experience. At the heart of it, people with disabilities are asking just to be treated normally with normal expectations. One man who has low sight explained that as he was exiting the restroom at work, a colleague held the door open for him. As he walked through the door, the colleague said, "Good job, buddy." He explains, "If his expectations of what I could do are so low that he thinks I need praise for walking out of the restroom, what are his expectations for me actually performing my job?"

While people want to be treated normally with normal expectations, there may be specific situations in which it would be nice to have a little help. A simple "Anything I can do to assist you?" goes a long way instead of assuming that people can't do something on their own or assuming that you know what kind of assistance they must need.

People will be happy to tell you what they need. A blind man that coauthor Baran was interviewing recently explained that when he is walking down the hall at work, people may try to silently get out of his way, pressing themselves up against the wall. Though their intentions are good, they are implicitly communicating, "You are a burden," to him. He asks that instead, people just say, "Hi, Bill," and the audible clues help him navigate the hall much easier and more normally. Another man with low sight added that if people say something like, "Hi, Bill; it's Carol," when passing in the hall, he can more quickly respond appropriately. Even if he knows Carol quite well, it can take a minute to process the sound of the voice, so by telling him your name, you help him greet you or maybe stop you to tell you something about work that he wanted to say before you've already passed each other in the hall.

EXAMPLE: "I'm deaf. I can read."

Hannah is deaf. She tells a story about how when she flies on an airplane, her ticket says "deaf" on it so that the crew knows, in case of emergency. She boards the plane first, and she often tells the flight attendants that if there is an emergency to make sure to tap her on the shoulder since she is deaf.

One time on a work trip, as people were boarding the plane, she felt a tap on her shoulder and the flight attendant handed her the emergency instructions card in braille. Think about that. What kind of subtle act of exclusion was happening here? The flight attendant was implicitly communicating, "You are invisible," in that she didn't actually see Hannah's specific situation. She was also communicating, "You are not an individual," in that she lumped Hannah into some general category of disability and gave her the one resource that she had for a disability, without thinking whether it applied to this particular person.

Hannah explains how she could have gotten angry but instead chose to respond to the flight attendant with humor. She rubbed the braille card on her ear and said, "Hmmm. Doesn't work." She then clarified that she is deaf but can read. Addressing the SAE in this way can be highly effective too, rather than not saying anything. Initiators may feel strong emotions for being so thoughtless. That's exactly what makes SAE accountability so effective for lasting behavior changes for the better.

Here are some additional example SAE:

- **You are not an individual**. While at a conference, Jay tries to network with other professionals. The ASL translator volunteers to be a proxy for Jay. As they make their rounds and have conversations, Jay starts to notice that the people he is talking to are only making eye contact and interacting with the translator, not Jay. These SAE additionally make him feel invisible, as he is literally not being seen when people only make eye contact with the translator. And while it is perhaps a natural instinct for people to look at the translator, a little practice and thought makes it so that Jay can feel seen and valued as an individual.

- **You are inadequate**. Sarah is a young woman who gets around in a wheelchair. While Sarah is at the mall, sales representatives keep asking her if she needs help reaching anything or trying on clothes. They would speak slowly and use an almost baby-talk tone of voice. Sarah knew they were trying to be helpful, but it came across as if they thought Sarah couldn't take care of herself and needed a stranger to help her try on a dress.

- **You're a threat**. Kris, a very fit, able-bodied man, goes to pick up his middle-school daughter from her theater audition. Kris is a mixed-race, muscular man with brown skin and tattoos. He is also a construction worker who left a worksite to get his daughter, so he was construction dusty. The chaperones who staffed the door were letting parents into the massive theater with no identification checks or questions. When Kris arrived at the glass door, they kept it locked and attempted to shoo him away. They certainly assumed he did not belong there, as most of the auditioning children were white. But they also saw him as a threat to everyone's safety, due to his physical stature and likely his race, so they denied him entrance.

Bias and discrimination can be complex and multifaceted. How might the chaperones have responded if the parent was a mom, or using a wheelchair? People often assume that body- and ability-based bias is always against those with special needs. Sometimes the height and strength of an able-bodied person is considered threatening. This is one of the premises behind the Black Lives Matter movement. Able-bodied Black men are considered a threat in the United States and far too often executed instead of approached with kindness and compassion.

- **You're a curiosity**. Bunny is a 6′3″ retired model with an amazing heart and an invisible disability. As a result, she requires the assistance of one or more service dogs. Her dogs are Great Danes due to Bunny's stature. Guinness, Titan, and her dearly departed Goose have all served her loyally and diligently as life-saving early warning signalers and walking canes. When her service dogs are working, it is usually clear because they wear service dog collars, even though they are not legally required to wear indicators. The service dog collars allow observant people to know that her assistants should not be petted or distracted. Nonetheless, people approach the animals, ask her a million questions, and incessantly disbelieve her disability status because she's tall, brilliant, stunning, and seemingly able-bodied. So she becomes a walking curiosity, endlessly pelted with questions and met with incredulity. Even as a professional disability advocate through her company Pawsible, she doesn't want to spend all day fielding questions about her ability status.

Notice the Dynamic

Let's look at a few ability-based SAE and see whether you can identify the operating dynamic based on the chapter 1 taxonomy.

- ► You are invisible.

- ► You are inadequate.

- ► You are not an individual.

- ► You don't belong.

- ► You are not normal.

- ► You are a curiosity.

- ► You are a threat.

- ► You are a burden.

Read each of the situations and think about what is happening. How might each group or individual be feeling?

- Situation 1: Always expecting a person using a wheelchair to look up at you when you could inconspicuously come down to their level.
    - What kind of SAE is happening?
    - How might the person in the wheelchair be feeling?
    - How might the able-bodied person be feeling?
    - How might the informed bystanders be feeling?
- Situation 2: A waiter sees a blind man sit down with his wife and children and asks the wife whether the man would like a menu in braille.
    - What kind of SAE is happening?
    - How might the blind man be feeling?
    - How might the waiter be feeling?
    - How might the man's family be feeling?
- Situation 3: Making a joke to someone in a wheelchair, like, "Watch out, you might get a speeding ticket!"
    - What kind of SAE is happening?
    - How might the person in the wheelchair be feeling?
    - How might the person making the joke be feeling?
    - How might the bystanders be feeling?
- Situation 4: Casually saying something like, "I'm so depressed; they ran out of chocolate," at a company ice cream social in front of someone who suffers from clinical depression.
    - What kind of SAE is happening?
    - How might the person who experiences the SAE be feeling?
    - How might the person who is upset about not getting chocolate ice cream be feeling?
    - How might the observers in the know be feeling?

- Situation 5: Asking someone with an invisible cognitive disability to read something quickly: "It's so easy, it will just take a minute."

  - What kind of SAE is happening?

  - How might the person who experiences the SAE be feeling?

  - How might the person who is making the request be feeling?

  - How might the observers in the know be feeling?

Here is how the taxonomy can be applied to these situations:

- Situation 1: Not taking time to make a small modification to your behavior can make some people feel **invisible**, as if you are trying to pretend not to see their circumstances. At the same time, do not make their situation your only focus or topic of discussion. You don't need to squat down next to them and draw even more attention to the circumstance. Instead, it's better to try and take a seat casually by pulling up a chair, if there is one close to you. Otherwise, squatting down can seem demeaning or even as if you are viewing them like a child. One man in a wheelchair tells the story of an example of feeling valued when he went into an Apple Store to shop for an iPad. The employee came over and, without making a big deal out of it, took the iPad off the counter and brought it down so he could test it out. That little gesture made him feel visible, respected, and normal.

- Situation 2: This assumes the person is **inadequate** and not even able to communicate about what he needs. He also likely feels **invisible**. The waiter was probably trying to be helpful, but as is the case with the example where the flight attendant didn't think about what it meant to be deaf, this waiter is not thinking about what it means to be specifically blind. In this case, the man's wife, who is used to situations like this, responded, "I don't know. Why don't you ask him?" She and the whole family are allies who witness these SAE frequently and share the burden of speaking up and educating people.

▸ Situation 3: The person making this joke is obviously not trying to do harm. In fact, they are trying to show comfort by speaking up in a casual joking manner, the way they might joke with someone else. Or they might be feeling discomfort and trying to alleviate that by making a joke. By leading with a joke or a comment about someone's disability, they are communicating that the person, as a person, is not **visible**, compared to their disability, which looms so largely visible. Observers who know the man in the wheelchair may be internally cringing because they see this happen over and over, with different variations. If they are trained in the SAE accountability system, they can feel empowered to speak up as an ally.

▸ Situation 4: Unlike situation 3, this may be a case where the speaker has no idea at all that the person they are talking to suffers from depression. It is an invisible disability, and the person who suffers from depression may want to hide that from people they work with, afraid that they will be treated as "less than"—not trusted with big projects, not given promotions, etc. In this case, the person who was wanting chocolate ice cream is not feeling anything unusual (aside from the totally understandable disappointment that they ran out of chocolate). They have no idea that their words can cause such strong emotions in someone. There may be a trusted coworker who is an observer and sees the impact of that word on their friend. But because this is not something that is open at work, the observer can't speak up as an ally. In that case, it would be better to check in on your friend privately later and see if there is any support you can give them.

▸ Situation 5: Like in situation 4, the person with an invisible cognitive disability, perhaps from a past stroke or head injury, might not be open about that disability with coworkers for fear of being treated differently. And they may struggle with some tasks that seem easy for others, especially when called on to do them quickly on the spot. So they might be strongly feeling **not normal** and **inadequate**. It's good for all people to recognize that more people than you think are walking around with invisible disabilities, and it's helpful to not make assumptions about what should be easy for others.

In sum, there are a wide variety of disabilities, physical and mental, that affect way more people than many of us realize. As such, it's good to think before speaking and acting in order to not make assumptions about what people can do, what they may feel, and what they may need. Treating people as normal, not making assumptions, and asking questions can go a long way toward making people of varying abilities feel included, at work and in other contexts.

8

Religion SAE

RELIGION IS AN INCREDIBLY INTERESTING domain to look at SAE, precisely because, for so many people, religion represents a deep, foundational way of seeing the world and how people should live in it. People believe deeply in their God or gods, their values, their communities, their practices, and their histories. Religion is central in many people's lives, and this is largely true across the globe and throughout recorded history.

Of course, not everyone has religious beliefs. Many people are atheists who don't believe there is a God. Many are agnostics, who don't have faith in religion but also aren't atheists. And even among those who do belong to an organized religion, there are varying degrees of belief. Some people are devout while others take part in many of the cultural practices but don't strictly follow the tenets of the religion. In complex, diverse societies like the United States, this makes for interesting and sometimes conflicting interactions, even in places that are not explicitly religious such as school and work.

Following the guidelines in this book, we argue that it is critical that workplaces be spaces where people can feel equally valued and respected no matter what their religious beliefs. And we believe that most people want to be accepting of others and their religious beliefs. However, this is another domain where people who are part of the dominant majority religion don't often have significant contact or experience with other religions. In the case of the United States, the dominant religion is Christianity in terms of numbers of people, but also in terms of influencing the culture, structuring work and school calendars, etc. Because of this, non-Christians may often be faced with subtle acts of exclusion communicating, "You are not normal," "You don't belong," and "You are invisible."

It may be natural to think that these SAE based on religion wouldn't be frequent in the workplace, but you may be surprised to hear how common they are, largely because of the way that religion forms the foundation of how even non-religious spaces are organized in the United States. In the following chapter, we give some examples of SAE that people may experience in the workplace in order to build understanding for the different realities that people experience. In these examples we explain some of the ways that addressing these religious SAE has turned out, and we propose some ways that it could go better, using the SAE accountability system described in chapter 3.

EXAMPLE: Yom Kippur: Why it's critical for individuals and leaders to speak up for SAE accountability

Let's take the example of David, a Jewish man working at a large company headquartered in the mid-Atlantic. This company would be considered progressive when it comes to diversity and inclusion. They take it very seriously. And yet, SAE still happen. David's job is high pressure. He works a lot on several different teams and several projects. Meetings that he needs to attend are constantly being scheduled, in addition to regular standing meetings.

Every year, David takes Yom Kippur off from work to fast and attend services with his family. Yom Kippur is generally considered to be the most holy day of all the Jewish holidays. It's blocked off on his shared calendar as a day off. David is somewhat resentful that he must use one of his vacation days to celebrate his holiday, but as a Jewish person, he is used to that, and he understands that it's hard to accommodate the holidays of every religion. He notices that the company calendar lists the holiday, which is nice, and David is hopeful that at least people will keep that in mind as they schedule meetings and think about deadlines.

Unfortunately, this year that doesn't happen. He notices that important meetings get scheduled for that day. David is then faced with three options. First, he could email the organizers of the meetings and ask that they reschedule. One of the meetings in particular involves a lot of people, and David really doesn't like to make waves like this. He knows people are busy, and he hates to give the organizers the extra work of finding a different day for the meeting. He knows he could do it, but he doesn't like that option.

Second, he could just miss the meeting; that's certainly an option. But he also doesn't like that option. He is trying hard to do a great job on this new project, and that meeting is a critical early-stage meeting. He knows that people will understand if he explains that he must miss it because of Yom Kippur. But he also knows, realistically, that people will hold it against him a little bit. He has seen it before in the way that people look at him or roll their eyes a little when he explains about missing work that day.

He really feels as if his only option is the third one—to try to join the meeting virtually from home, even on his day off. One of the meetings on his calendar he will just have to miss, but this other one he could likely join after services but before heading to his aunt's house for break-the-fast dinner. It's not a great option either, as he really likes to unplug and concentrate on his family and his religion during this day, but it feels to him as if he must make this tradeoff. It makes his identity feel less important than others', and he speculates about how people would respond if it was ever suggested that they do a meeting on Christmas, for example.

This year, David is frustrated enough about the situation that he does talk openly about it with some people at work. He's just making casual conversation. But one day he happens to be talking about it with someone who's on the D&I council, and this person sees that David is not feeling included at work because of the situation. The D&I council person, Shannon, sees this as important and writes the chair of the council and the chief diversity officer. Both of these people take the concern seriously and quickly get in touch with David and Shannon. They ask about which meeting was specifically causing a problem. Within 24 hours, that meeting has been rescheduled.

Was this a good outcome? Was it good for David? Was it good for others at the organization? Did it build more of an inclusive culture at the organization? These are important questions to consider, especially from the point of view of what **individuals can do** about SAE and what **HR or leaders can do** about SAE when they happen. David at first felt a mix of emotions. On the one hand, he was certainly relieved and grateful that he could take the day completely off to observe the holiday without interruption. And he was appreciative of the swift action taken by his colleagues. He felt as if they were concerned about him and took care of him. However, he also felt bad that he had put people out, and he felt out of the loop.

He was worried about how the situation had been handled and how his name might have been used. Did the council chair reprimand the meeting organizer? David certainly didn't want that and would have been especially mortified if they had done it while using him as the reason. He was apprehensive now about his interpersonal relationship with that person. Was it going to be awkward? He didn't know if he should bring it up or not. By not including him in the conversation, trust and understanding weren't built among the employees involved.

And there was another reason why David was not thrilled with how the situation was handled. While David was individually taken care of, he didn't feel as though the deeper issue was addressed. He imagined there were lots of other religious minorities who had the same or similar issues, and their situation hadn't been improved at all. He felt as if an opportunity had been missed to (1) create understanding so that this kind of thing could be avoided in the future and (2) make all religious minorities feel valued, even though their holidays were not going to be company-wide days off.

What are the lessons? How could things have gone differently using the SAE accountability system? David, as an individual, was reluctant to speak up originally and say something to the organizer of the meeting. He saw speaking up as just something negative that would have created work for people who would have unconsciously held it against him. However, if his whole organization had been trained and practiced speaking up as an opportunity to learn, grow, build trust, and create inclusion, he would have felt less anxious about saying something. He would have known that his speaking up was part of a larger endeavor and journey that the organization was doing together. When he spoke up and was positively rewarded for it, he would have felt trust being built with meeting organizers and would have felt that he was helping to create a culture of inclusion that could potentially carry over to people of all sorts of marginalized identities.

Shannon, the D&I council member, also felt that her colleagues in D&I missed an opportunity. She wondered what would have happened if the D&I office had worked with HR to send a communication out to the entire organization. A month before the holiday, they could have sent an email saying something to the effect of, "Yom Kippur is the most holy day for Jewish people, a day when people don't eat or drink anything and a day when people atone for their sins throughout the year and are cleansed. While we don't mark this as an official company day off, we ask that you appreciate that many of your colleagues will be taking the day off, and we ask that you try to avoid scheduling important meetings for this day." A clear communication like this would help prevent meetings from being scheduled in the first place and would therefore make it so that individuals didn't have to figure out how to respond to the SAE on their own. It communicates a message of inclusion to the entire organization.

Similarly, a message like this could go out in advance of the most holy and most celebrated days of all major religions. While you can never address all holidays for all religions, communicating about the most important ones creates a culture of inclusion and an understanding that helps everyone adapt to the organization calendar, which is specifically organized around holidays of the dominant religion.

EXAMPLE: December holidays

Ari finds the December holiday season to be full of subtle acts of exclusion. It begins in early December as the office gets decorated. There is a nod toward Hanukkah, as a little lighted menorah is placed on the counter, but of course the decorations are almost exclusively celebrating Christmas, as is the music being played in the lobby. Ari is used to this and even understands it from a "numbers" perspective.

There are more Christians in his workplace, and Christmas is a much bigger deal to Christians than Hanukkah is to Jewish people. It's more the stuff that people say that he considers the subtle acts of exclusion. As Christmas gets closer, lots of people end conversations, calls, and emails with "Happy holidays!" or

"Hope you have a great holiday!" But many also just say, "Merry Christmas!" and every time, he tries to decide whether to just go with it or to explain that he doesn't celebrate Christmas. People making assumptions that everyone celebrates Christmas makes him feel invisible, but he also doesn't want to have conversations about it all the time.

One example really sticks in his mind. It was December 24th during a year when Christmas and Hanukkah were overlapping (they don't always overlap because Hanukkah follows the Jewish calendar). Ari and his team had a hard deadline to get a report finished before the Christmas holiday, so they were working late and finally finished around 5:30 p.m. Ari and his colleague headed out to the parking lot together. As they were saying goodbye, the colleague gave an awkward smile and said, "Happy Hanukkah," but with a sort of rising tone as if it were a question. Ari said, "Thanks!" (feeling considered) and then the colleague said in a very earnest voice, "But seriously, man, Merry Christmas," and put out his hand for a handshake.

This SAE really made Ari feel invisible, as his true identity (the one that celebrates Hanukkah) was treated as not quite real or even a curiosity in the mind of his colleague. As Ari tells it, it's not that he felt so bad about it in the moment, and in fact he tells the story often and gets big laughs out of it. This is important to realize, as initiators may hold onto a subject's response of "It doesn't bother me" or "I'm not offended" to rationalize or excuse the SAE. Subjects have learned to cope with SAE in a wide variety of ways, including working hard to not let SAE bother them and not getting in big discussions about them every time. Initiators need to understand that one subject's brushing off of an SAE does not make it fair game to continue doing that SAE.

Regarding this example, it's clearly not just Jewish people who experience these SAE communicating that their religious identity and beliefs are not visible or valid. People treating anyone's religion or faith (even Christians) as not really real would be considered subtle acts of exclusion.

EXAMPLE: An atheist's dilemma: Prayer before work meetings

Sebastian works at a small company with strong values and a tight leadership, all of which is fairly religious. They are all Christian, and they believe that Christian values underlie the mission of the organization and the guidelines for how to treat one another at work. Team meetings at the organization begin with a short prayer. Sebastian really enjoys the work that he is doing, and he believes in the mission. But he is a committed atheist and doesn't feel comfortable with the praying in the workplace.

He feels as if he must hide his beliefs to go with the flow in the organization. He looked up the legality of this and found that it seems legal as long as they excuse people who don't want to participate and as long as there is no retaliation or repercussion for not participating. And while he knows that they would not likely explicitly retaliate, he does feel as if his chances for being promoted to senior leadership would be lower if he were to speak up. He is truly at a loss for what to do.

The authors have seen this sort of situation not only at small companies, but also at large corporations where the leadership is perceived as culturally and religiously homogeneous and people are afraid that if they don't conform, they will not be as likely to be promoted to senior leadership. In these larger companies, the SAE isn't something as explicit as prayer before meetings, but is more subtle things that people say, such as making small talk by asking what church people attend, or asking what people did to celebrate Christmas or Easter.

In Sebastian's case, speaking up as an individual without a leadership training component does in fact come with significant personal risk. While he could speak up tactfully and kindly about the praying, there is a decent chance that at least subconsciously this could impact the way that he is viewed by leadership. Before that happens, it's critical that leaders understand just why inclusion is so important to their organization and how something like prayer can exclude people. As discussed in chapter 4, once leaders deeply understand why inclusion is important, why their organization will benefit from diverse perspectives, and what their role as leaders should be, they will be able to assess organizational practices like this one and understand its impacts on inclusion. Even seemingly inclusive modifications like praying without specific mention of any particular religion will still be an SAE to people like Sebastian who are atheists.

EXAMPLE: Religion, politics, and Islam

Zara is a practicing Muslim woman who wears a hijab to work at her large office in Minneapolis. She is in her twenties and didn't experience life in the workplace immediately after September 11, 2001. Since she started her job five years ago, she has always encountered SAE in the workplace, as people ask her questions about her hijab and her religion that make her feel as if she doesn't belong, she is a threat, and she is a curiosity. With the election and presidency of Donald Trump, Zara has simultaneously found more support from people, and also more subtle acts of exclusion. And the SAE that she encounters are different and more confusing than ever.

One day she walked into John's office for a meeting. On his desk was an American flag and a framed picture of President Trump. She found it hard to concentrate on what they were discussing, looking at that photo and checking in with her feelings. This was early 2017, not long after Trump had signed an executive order banning foreign nationals from seven predominantly Muslim countries from entering the country for ninety days.

This was popularly known as the Muslim ban. Zara herself was born in the United States and has family in Somalia, one of the countries listed on the ban. She feels strongly hurt and excluded. And yet, she also feels confused. Her colleague hadn't said anything offensive to her. He simply had a picture of the president of the United States on his desk. She didn't know if he endorsed those particularly damaging things that the president had said or done that not so subtly communicated that she and people like her were a threat.

Zara didn't say anything about this to John. In fact, she didn't say anything about it to anyone at the office. She honestly felt such a strong mix of anger, confusion, sadness, and dread that she was really struggling to work with John or others that she knew or suspected to be supporters of the president. She logically knew that there were many varied reasons that people may have had for supporting a politician. She also logically knew that many people support a president no matter what they say or what party they are from. And yet to her, what was happening with the travel ban felt unprecedented and, frankly, as if it went against the company's as well as the country's values. She didn't know how John could be so clueless about how she would feel with that picture staring back at her. Or maybe he did know and just didn't care. Either way, she felt incredibly uncomfortable, as if she didn't belong in her own workplace.

This felt different. There were many other SAE over the years that Zara and other Muslims she knew had spoken up about at work. When catered lunches for company functions heavily contained pork, they spoke up and the company happily provided plenty of non-pork options at future lunches. When Zara and a couple of others requested a dedicated prayer space so that they could pray during the workday, they were met with some subtle resistance but eventually were able to secure a clean space. During these other instances, it felt that the SAE being communicated were "You are not normal" and "You are a burden." Those felt bad for sure, but nothing compared to the "You are a threat" SAE that Zara occasionally feels, now more than ever.

Even diversity and inclusion practitioners like the authors struggle with the best way to approach SAE like this. We all know that it's important to respect people's political beliefs. And we know that political beliefs have certainly always impacted different groups in disproportionate ways. And we know that people in high political office have often said things that were offensive or subtle acts of exclusion. Yet, what's a D&I practitioner to do with the political statements that are directly contrary to the values of diversity and inclusion? It is especially during these times that we recommend following the SAE accountability guidelines in this book.

These are critical for bringing people together during such polarizing political times and connecting over challenging conversations rather than growing farther apart. We won't pretend that will be easy to do, but following guidelines such as assuming good intent, replacing defensiveness with curiosity and empathy, and listening actively are our best hope for truly connecting across these polarizing differences in ideology.

In conclusion, religion can be challenging because of the way it encompasses deeply held beliefs about some of the most serious issues humans grapple with—mortality, faith, culture, how to be a good person, etc. A minority of people can't even get to the place of respecting other religions' right to exist, in which case they are unlikely to be concerned with understanding these subtle acts of exclusion. But we believe that most people respect the beliefs of others and will be willing to learn and grow.

9

Age and Generation SAE

"GENERATIONS" ARE A WAY of imposing categorical boundaries around something that is inherently a linear spectrum (when people were born). Yet, like some other categories of difference, people form ideas around these categories and then develop biases in the way they relate to others. Age/generation is an interesting dimension of identity to consider for SAE because everyone alive today has been younger before, and if people are fortunate enough to live a long, full life, they will also experience being older. This is unlike other dimensions of identity where most people have different experiences that don't overlap. Sure, some people may experience being both able-bodied and disabled, or may experience living as heterosexual for a time and gay for a time. But for most people, if you identify as Black, you aren't going to experience being white, and if you identify as a man you aren't going to experience life identifying as a woman.

That fact, that we all experience different ages, is what differentiates age from generation. We can relate to the different experiences and commonalities of age, but we still stereotype people based on our ideas about generational difference. Different people may have biases for or against others based on whether they perceive them to be of the same or a different generation. And while bias may exist against people of any age or generation, those ages most marginalized in the workplace tend to be those perceived to be young and those perceived to be old.

Starting in 2016, millennials became the largest single generation in the workplace.[1] And yet, it is still acceptable for people to openly express stereotypes and biases against this entire generation of over seventy million people in the US alone. Scrolling through LinkedIn recently, one author found several postings of videos trying to be funny by simulating a "millennial job interview" and scenarios of things "millennials say at work." You've probably seen these videos, or if you haven't, you likely know the stereotypes they are playing on: millennials are lazy, are entitled, can't wake up early or work hard, need constant praise, can only interact via smartphone, etc. Ironically, putting a slightly more positive spin on all these stereotypes turns them into some business best practices quite easily. For example, millennials

- understand that mental health is important for long term happiness and satisfaction, in life and in work;

- understand that feedback should be frequent and should point out strengths as well as opportunities for improvement;

- are sensitive to subtle acts of exclusion in the workplace and point them out when they happen;

- are in touch with the changing business environment and have the skills to adapt to conditions.

Nonetheless, biases against this generation and Gen Z remain strong among older generations. And on the other end of the spectrum, baby boomers and folks who are perceived as older also frequently experience subtle acts of exclusion. These may include the following:

- joking about an older person's lack of ability or experience with anything digital, technical, or social media related

- referencing or joking about older people having failing memories, poor eyesight or hearing, an inability to have sex, or other physical failings

- patronizing older people with a loud, slow, or high pitched voice

Although most people know that they must check these age/generation biases in the workplace, subtle acts of exclusion like these are still common. Some examples follow.

EXAMPLE: "You're not like other millennials."

Claire, a twenty-three-year-old college graduate with a degree in marketing, is recently hired for an entry level job at an advertising agency. Over her first few weeks, she is thrown into several projects and is enjoying the work and the people. She really helps the team with some deliverables that they had been behind on. Her staff manager, Victoria, invites her out to lunch one day to thank her for the great work she is doing. As they eat, Victoria tells Claire what a fantastic job she is doing and how happy everyone is that she has joined the team. Victoria says, "We're just so lucky to have found you. You're not like other millennials. It's really challenging to find young people that really understand how to work hard."

Claire thanks Victoria for the compliment. But she feels uneasy about Victoria's SAE, saying that young people don't know how to work hard. It's a biased way of thinking about her generation that she knows isn't true. What was supposed to be a celebratory lunch has now made her feel worried and apprehensive about other biases that Victoria and others at the agency may have about young people. She doesn't say anything because she is new and doesn't want to rock the boat. She later wonders what she could have said in that moment. She knows the stereotypes that people have about millennials. She has even heard people mutter "millennial" under their breath as an insult, even when someone is making a great suggestion to improve the workplace.

Victoria thinks she is giving a compliment, as is the case with many SAE; however, it has an unintended message that Claire (and others of her generation) is inadequate. We have seen people make these SAE right in the middle of our diversity and inclusion workshops. Of course, we don't let them slide! We sometimes ask who in the room is a millennial. When many of the hands go up, people are often surprised. We ask, "Are these people lazy and entitled?" People will often say, "No, of course not; not these people." Then the light starts to go on that they may be unfairly holding a bias against a huge group of people.

As adults grow older in a rapidly changing society, there have always been those who grumble and complain about the "youth of today" and romanticize the past. We encourage people to not fall into that trap, but rather to approach different generations with curiosity and empathy. And we encourage people to be pragmatic. If millennials are the largest generation in the workforce, are you going to change that? Are you going to change them? Or are you going to better understand them, to leverage their talent for the organization, create inclusive workplaces where they can thrive and connect better with customers of that same generation?

EXAMPLE: "When is he going to retire?"

Jim was a sixty-five-year-old salesperson at an automobile company. He had been working there for seven years, and it had not gone smoothly. Jim had been written up several times for poor performance and had been given overall low performance evaluations. During the manager meeting discussing performance evaluations and possible compensation increases, the managers were discussing what to do about Jim. One of the managers, Carlos, asked, "When is he going to retire?"

Carlos meant the question literally. He was wondering whether the other managers had information about Jim retiring because that could impact the decision about what to do regarding his poor performance. As soon as he said it, however, he realized it wasn't appropriate to say, even though Jim was not in the room. He didn't have the exact words, but he knew that what he said could be interpreted as implying that Jim's poor performance was because he was older.

In that moment, Carlos froze. He just ignored his own comment and hoped that everyone else ignored it too. But in the coming weeks, he had a sinking feeling in his stomach, wondering if he would be written up or even disciplined for what he knew was inappropriate. If he and his colleagues could have practiced SAE accountability, they might have been able to discuss this productively in the moment instead.

Notice the Dynamic

Let's look at some more age-based SAE and see whether you can identify the operating dynamic based on the chapter 1 taxonomy.

- ► You are invisible.
- ► You are inadequate.
- ► You are not an individual.
- ► You don't belong.
- ► You are not normal.
- ► You are a curiosity.
- ► You are a threat.
- ► You are a burden.

Read each situation and think about what is happening. How might each group or individual be feeling?

- ▸ Situation 1: Linda is a fifty-five-year-old woman who is applying to a managerial position at a tech company. This company is primarily composed of employees who are thirty-five years old or younger. Linda has a BA and a master's degree in tech development and is qualified for the job. She went through three rounds of interviews, but ultimately did not get the job. When Linda asked why—in hopes of improving on the issue as she continued to look for a job—the interviewer said she just wasn't a good "culture fit."

- ▸ Situation 2: Tammy is applying for a new job. The company accepts only online applications. As Tammy comes to the application's education section, she realizes that the latest college graduation year listed is 1980. Tammy graduated in 1978, so she is confused as to what to do. She ends up not applying for the job.

- ▸ Situation 3: Jamie, a twenty-year-old senior in college, was talking with his supervisor at his internship position. They were discussing the issue of systemic racism in the United States. Jamie's supervisor laughed at Jamie's comparison of modern school segregation to the legal segregation of the past. He said, "You're too young to have any idea what that was like," and dismissed his comments. Jamie felt as if he had made a mistake with his information and was appearing unintelligent.

- ▸ Situation 4: Rose is a twenty-two-year-old college graduate. She has a degree in journalism and marketing. During her college career she held several leadership roles on campus and participated in internships and volunteer opportunities to build up her resume. Now that she has graduated, she is looking for a full-time job, but because her experience was mostly unpaid, potential employers aren't viewing her efforts as professional. She has been offered several unpaid internships, but has not been given the chance to prove she can navigate a professional environment while holding a full-time position.

- Situation 5: Bob is a sixty-eight-year-old man who is looking for a part-time job to stay busy during his "retirement." He worked for forty-five years in accounting and is looking to stay in that field. He goes on several interviews and notices that every time he checks in with the receptionist they comment on how "cute" or "adorable" or "handsome" he looks in his suit.

Here is how the taxonomy can be applied to these situations:

- Situation 1: When we limit our professional and business development efforts to a matter of culture, we are neglecting the true value of a person: their skills. Linda felt as if **she didn't belong** in this space because of her age, and that is why she didn't get the job. Using inclusive hiring practices, such as blind resume audits, can prevent losing the perfect candidate due to unconscious bias.

- Situation 2: Subtle acts of exclusion don't always have to be face to face. By setting your preferences on online applications to inadvertently not allow people of a certain age group to apply, you send the message that these people are **invisible**. Make sure you give all applicants the opportunity to complete their applications in full.

- Situation 3: This comment not only made Jamie second guess himself, it made him feel as if he shouldn't contribute to the conversation or continue to learn about this issue. Feeling **inadequate** can lead to apathy, which can prevent people from reaching their full potential and making a positive difference. Try to avoid making demeaning comments when talking with people in different age groups.

- Situation 4: Being told the years of work she has done to better herself and her community aren't "professional" or "actual" work experience tells Rose that she's **not visible** and not important. The work she has done was legitimate. When interviewing candidates or talking with younger professionals, express the validity of the work they've done and see it as the professional investment it is.

▸ Situation 5: No one likes to be diminished based on their appearance. When applying for a job, you especially don't want the first thing people think about you to be that you are less than a full professional person. Seeing a job applicant as a candidate, instead of an age or a stereotype, is paramount to a successful interview. It can be belittling to be called cute or even handsome for trying to support yourself and your family. It makes you feel **inadequate**.

In the following pages, we present to you a real-life example of an SAE based on age that recently happened to coauthor Jana during the writing of this book. We describe the SAE and the response in detail, which we can do because it happened over email. We want to present you with the whole exchange and walk you through how it follows the guidelines of the SAE accountability system so that you can see how it plays out in real life, not only in hypothetical situations. Coauthor Jana describes the exchange:

> During the writing of this book, someone read my third book, the second edition of *The B Corp Handbook: How to Use Business as a Force for Good*. The person who read the book owns a B Corp (B Corps are purpose-driven companies that create benefit for all stakeholders, not just shareholders) and is a member of the B Corp community. I had originally come to coauthor the second edition after being a case study in the first edition of the same book. I was invited by the original author, Ryan Honeyman, to coauthor the second edition through the lens of diversity, equity, and inclusion. Ryan happens to be a cisgender white man, so he sought an expert of color to expand on how and why B Corps

should embed DEI policies and practices into their businesses. The book was an instant best seller and the response to the new angle was overwhelmingly positive.

The B Corp business owner who read the book, however, wrote to me with the following mixed feedback:

First of all, I wanted to thank you and Ryan for collaborating on a great second edition of the B Corp Handbook. I am getting a lot out [of] the update!

While reading your passionate and articulate Intro I became aware that ageism was not explicitly mentioned. I wondered if this may be a blind spot[2] for you, given your age? In my mind, this is a major issue in diversity that is currently being overshadowed. "Seniors" are being marginalized in the workplace while, ironically, we are at our peak of experience and wisdom. In reality, we have great contributions to make to organizations and are still "mid-life" given today's longevity. Chip Conley speaks eloquently about ageism and best represents our voice when he talks and writes about the Modern Elder and Wisdom at Work.[3] I believe ageism largely an unconscious and unspoken bias.

If you'd like to reach out and communicate further, I'd welcome it.

The email was addressed to me, but Ryan also received a copy and intervened as an ally before I had a chance:

Thanks for the note. Dr. Jana most definitely does not have a blindspot around ageism. We spoke about it a few times while writing the B Corp Handbook 2nd edition. They know that there are lots of different areas of discrimination and unconscious bias in our culture.

However, part of what we are trying to do with the Second Edition of the book was center the experiences of people of color (particularly Black and Indigenous folks). We wanted to talk about how the delusion of white supremacy (that we are steeped in in our culture) affects our work in the B Corp community and society more broadly.

I know you aren't arguing this, but ageism in no way compares to 400 years of enslavement, oppression, and violence that Black folks suffered (and continue to suffer) at the hands of white folks. Older white men like Chip Conley still have VAST amounts of privilege that age will never take away from them.

I acknowledge that it is a slippery slope when trying to go down the "my oppression is greater than your oppression" wormhole. It's called the "oppression olympics" and doesn't get us to a place of shared empathy and understanding.

That's why we believe that naming, disrupting, and dismantling white supremacy is the most important thing we can do in the B Corp community. White supremacy is the magician behind the curtain affecting everything we do in our culture. It is the driver for all of this.

I also have to level with you. You also have to be careful writing to an expert in the field of DEI that you don't know (especially a Black gender non-conforming expert in DEI who has experienced white supremacy on a level that we white folks will never understand) and [telling] them they might have a blindspot about ageism. It's an innocent question and you probably are genuinely interested. But there is a difference between **intent** and **impact**. You had a curious, genuine intention, but you made some assumptions that Dr. Jana might find offensive.

I have not talked to them, but if I got this email, I might think "who are you to tell me I have a blind spot? You don't know me." It is not an excuse that our intent is "good" or not.

A more appropriate question to submit to Dr. Jana might be "Hi, I love your work. I wanted to ask how you see ageism fitting into the discussion about DEI in the B Corp community? I am in no way trying to equate ageism with other more pernicious forms of oppression. I am just curious for your thoughts on ageism so that I can learn more. Any resources you might be able to direct me to would be very helpful."

As you can tell, I am very passionate about this topic. If you are interested in learning more about my thoughts on this, check out my article: White People: Let's Talk About White Supremacy.[4] I would encourage you to reach out to me with any further questions, as Dr. Jana is very busy and I don't want to add more content to [their] inbox.

Ryan Honeyman

I was blown away by the vocal support. My staff had also fielded the email in advance and warned me that it was coming. Both of these are examples of guideline 1 for SAE observers and subjects—**pause the action**. Allies ensconced me and interrupted the microaggression before it could even cause me any dismay. Both allies **assumed good intent** (guideline 2) in their correspondence. Ryan **explained** to the reader exactly **why he had paused the action**—guideline 3. Ryan's approach was effective, because before I could even respond, I received the following email from the original reader:

Hello again Tiffany (Dr. Jana),

After sending my email yesterday, I received feedback from Ryan that you and he intentionally focused on issues related to white supremacy and that you were well aware of ageism. He also mentioned that my assumptions and communication could be perceived as presumptuous and even disrespectful. The possibility of this left me somewhat unsettled and distressed. So, please accept my sincere apology if I caused any negative impact.

Again, I am in great appreciation of your work and Ryan's work.

Best regards,

Ryan's speaking up and holding the reader accountable for the SAE was effective. The reader could have skulked away angrily, but he didn't. This is a great example of guideline 1 for SAE initiators—**acknowledge feedback with gratitude**. He moved toward the discomfort, so I reciprocated:

Thanks for reaching back out. I didn't have time to be offended because my allies fielded everything for me—so your second message came through on the heels of the first with both warning (from my team) and intervention (from Ryan).

I am not one to harbor ill-will against people, nor assume the worst. I am fine and I thank you for the consideration of your second email and for the work that YOU do!

For what it's worth, my company has a budding partnership with the Department of [Aging] precisely because it is such an important issue. Nonetheless, what Ryan said about the identities we chose to center in the book is correct. I cannot cover all of the "isms" at the same time nor do I aim to please everyone. I allow my spirit to guide the words I speak and write in the moments and the forums that I am given.

I trust that the people who need them will find them, and I release them into the world.

As far as my age, I am old enough to be a grand-mother, with children old enough to have children. So were I to sue for age discrimination, I would be suing based on the fact that I am well over 40. ☺ Funny where blind spots can lurk....

In all seriousness, I didn't have time to be offended and I mean you no harm whatsoever. I trust we will all learn and grow from this interaction and advance in love and light.

♥ Grace and Peace ♥

    Tiffany Jana

What followed this exchange was a series of beautiful, heartfelt messages of affirmation, apology, forgiveness, and acceptance:

Thank you for communicating and being so generous of heart. My actions and the ripple it created has really caused me to take pause and reflect... to be more thoughtful and less impulsive.

Laura actually replied to me and informed me of the work on ageism TMI is undertaking. Great to hear!

Indeed, you can't address all the "isms" at the same time or to the same degree. Again, this has served as quite a learning experience for me.

I resonate with your words "I allow my spirit to guide the words I speak and write in the moments and the forums that I am given. I trust that the people who need them will find them, and I release them into the world". I've been slowly and awkwardly learning to navigate life using my inner guidance, the spirit within me.

Grace and peace to you

Without ever having read this book (because it was being written!), he **replaced defensiveness with curiosity**—guideline 2 for SAE initiators. Some of this work is intuitive and can become second nature once you get used to it and really invite it into your thinking and way of being.

What started with an SAE about my adequacy (via my professionalism and age) ended as a beautiful, teachable moment marked with an air of mutual respect. I **had patience but expected progress**—guideline 4 for observers and subjects.

Hearing that Spirit is growing in you and guiding you more and more, is the most wonderful thing I could hear. It's so easy for us to get wrapped up in human doing and human reacting. Spirit was placed within us to guide us, connect us, and offer us peace. The sooner and more consistently we all reconnect to source—the better for all life in the universe and beyond.

What a blessed exchange.

Thank you 🙏

We found common ground in our spirituality amid what could have become a bitter exchange. This was the final note from the reader who **followed through and followed up**—guideline 3 for SAE initiators:

Amen! Bless you for your open heart Tiffany.

That situation could have ended very differently. Note that my and Ryan's responses may not have been perfect—there is no such thing as a perfect response. The important thing is that we both moved toward the situation and stayed engaged. SAE accountability can be very effective. You just have to keep practicing and building your new muscles.

10

Intentional Acts of Inclusion

NOW THAT YOU UNDERSTAND the nature and pervasiveness of SAE, you will begin to see them everywhere. You will see people committing them all around you. You may even start to catch yourself before someone else can speak up. These are good things. This is an indication of the mindset shift we mentioned in the introduction. Just know that the nature of all diversity, equity, and inclusion work is that it truly is perpetual effort that good natured people choose to take on for a lifetime. Remember that the mindset shift is the beginning and the lasting impact happens as your behaviors are informed by that mental shift. When you find yourself making new choices and *behaving* more intentionally, inclusively, and like an ally—you have leveled up.

What Else Can I Do?

You may still be asking yourself, "Where do I go from here?" There are many places to start. Individuals can begin the personal work described in chapters 2 and 3 of this book to be more prepared to address SAE when they inevitably happen. Organizations can strategize for ways they can support individuals and create a culture where speaking up is encouraged and even celebrated (chapter 4).

In addition to that, everyone can step up their own proactive use of **intentional acts of inclusion**. By reading this book, you have taken a significant step toward becoming more intentionally inclusive. Reading this book is an intentional act of inclusion because of its promotion of action-oriented, ally behavior. It's even more inclusive if you act on what you have read. The next step is to really think about what you learned here and lean into the sometimes uncomfortable space of discussions about ally behavior and cultural fluency. When the subjects of diversity, equity, and inclusion come up, move toward the discussion instead of away from it. Learn to be comfortable owning that you are a student of life, ready and willing to learn more about that which you do not fully understand. Approach it with humility and an open heart.

Continue to seek out books and other resources that offer information on aspects of inclusion and culture about which you remain less familiar or less comfortable. Netflix has supported a few remarkable films that present hard-hitting facts and dramatizations about the United States and the world that most people have little familiarity with. For example, Ava DuVernay directed *When They See Us* and *13th* as great expositions of bias and subtle and overt acts of exclusion in the US justice system.

There are an endless stream of movies, books, and television shows that can offer windows into the world of people different from you. The challenge is that most of us continuously pursue media and resources that are comfortable, familiar reflections of our existing values versus those we may aspire to embody. Try diversifying your media watching, your news sources, your podcasts, your book authors, and your leisure activities. Listen to others' voices not from a place of judgment but from their perspective.

Intentional acts of inclusion can become part of the way you live your life. Holding space for people by seeing, acknowledging, and inviting underrepresented voices, bodies, and perspectives into the rooms you occupy is a particularly powerful choice. Leveraging your privilege to ensure that people with divergent views and experiences are being heard and taken seriously helps foster a sense of belonging. Of course, speaking up using the system we outline in this book is an intentional act of inclusion. Intentional acts of inclusion can be subtle or overt. Mentoring and sponsoring underrepresented people are overt acts of inclusion. If you are motivated and courageous enough to move directly into overt acts of inclusion—do it!

Intentional acts of inclusion don't have to be massive displays of magnanimity. For instance, a white man recently let coauthor Jana ahead of him to pay for snacks at a gas station.

> He arrived first at the register that opened up but noticed that I had been at the end of another longer line. Seems like no big deal, right? One could say he did the right thing because I was technically ahead of him if you consider my wait in the other line. But he had no real obligation to extend the courtesy. And I can tell you from forty-plus years on the planet that the courtesy is often not extended to Black people in similar situations. That may sound really petty, but trust me, it's true.
>
> His small but intentional act of inclusion was recognizing that he could have maintained his lead in the line but chose to invite me forward. My reciprocal act of inclusion was accepting the gracious act and simply thanking him for the kind gesture. I know a lot of people who would not have accepted it, but I recognized the spirit of inclusion and allowed him to count that as one point for inclusion and a hit against patriarchy and the delusion of white supremacy. Again, these things seem like minutia in isolation but add up to a greater construct of either inclusive or exclusive behavior that ultimately shapes the world we live in.

Intentional acts of inclusion at work don't have to require a huge effort or be very costly. Noticing that someone isn't participating in a discussion and inviting their opinion is an intentional act of inclusion. Putting your phone in your pocket and listening actively to a colleague as they tell you a personal story is an intentional act of inclusion. Sitting with someone outside your usual network at lunch can be an intentional act of inclusion. Giving credit and supporting people's growth and development in an organization can be an intentional act of inclusion. Once you get in the habit of making these intentional acts (micro-affirmations, as they are sometimes called), they come easier and easier, until it is second nature and you can't imagine a different way of moving through your workplace or the world.

Reach In to Reach Out

Being human is not as easy as we might hope. Being an intentionally kind, considerate human is even more challenging. But we believe that all of us have within ourselves the distinct ability to exceed our own limitations. Because the truth about this work is that if we ignore it or willfully opt out, we tacitly choose to live our lives selfishly and without care or concern for the well-being of the people we encounter.

And it's not just the stranger on the street or the casual acquaintance we are likely to offend, it's also the people closest to us—the family members or friends whose silent struggles we don't know or comprehend; the colleagues whose diversity we can't see but on whom we rely for peaceful, productive workdays and collaborative solutions; the clients whose values are more inclusive than our own and whose business we need to survive.

Whether you are an individual who read this book in search of guidance for becoming a more inclusive person, or someone in a leadership position, speaking up and supporting SAE accountability is one of the most effective choices you can make toward making the world a better place. Embracing these concepts and more importantly, changing your behaviors, will increase the psychological safety of those around you and likely expand your circle of friends and allies.

Consider the email Ryan Honeyman responded to when he witnessed an SAE initiated against coauthor Jana. Ryan could have easily remained a silent bystander via email and lost nothing. He's an author looking to sell books and a consultant with a business to run. He may have seen it in his own best interest to keep his criticism and strong, sometimes unpopular, opinions to himself.

Most of us want to preserve the status quo for fear of losing something—be it our livelihood, our reputation, or just our momentary peace of mind. Avoiding conflict is a common impulse. Yet what is the true cost of maintaining the status quo? When we fail to speak up, we tacitly agree with whatever was said. In Ryan's case, coauthor Jana had no idea Ryan received the same email, so he might have slipped off the hook unbeknownst to them. In speaking up, Ryan deepened his friendship with Jana, gained even more respect from them, and also gained more respect for himself and Jana from the reader by holding him accountable. The reader did not want to be offensive, so he was embarrassed but grateful to have the chance to not look inconsiderate.

Your gut will tell you when to act. Just listen to it. Stand up for SAE subjects when they are excluded. Some of us have become accustomed to suppressing the voice that tells us something isn't right. We all have an instinct that tells us when what we heard, saw, or witnessed was wrong. If for some reason you have lost your connection to that instinct, that internal moral barometer, you need to work on reconnecting it. Get quiet. Start taking time to meditate or just listen to what is happening inside you. Shut out the noise and be present to your thoughts, feelings, and experiences. This will help you make better, stronger connections to the beings around you.

Sometimes we want to intervene but we talk ourselves out of it. Fear dominates over integrity and compassion. We must allow empathy to rise to the top of our impulses and inform our actions. Focus on people when you are with them. Try to extend your feelings out into space to meet theirs. See if you can sense what they are feeling. It may sound crazy, but it will help you reconnect to the people around you who want to be there for you when you need them as well.

Our Vision for the Future

If the sum total of all our inclusive and exclusive choices shapes our reality, imagine the following possibility. Imagine a world where people no longer assume the worst about others based on how they look, act, or sound. Imagine a world full of thoughtful people who consider the impact of their words and actions before releasing them into the universe. In that world, equity becomes reality. Race, gender, class, age, ability, and dozens of other demographic characteristics cease to limit and define people's success, future, access, income, dreams, hopes, and outcomes. People are encouraged and expected to be exactly who they are.

Each of us has the power to make others feel

- you are enough,
- you are an individual,
- you belong,
- you are normal,
- you are special,
- you are safe.

Let's explore the beauty in the diversity of the human experience and wholeheartedly exclaim to each other

- I see you.
- I see you for who you are, what you bring, where you've been, and where you are from. All of you is perfect just the way you are.

Wouldn't things feel different if we were each greeted with that kind of open-hearted acceptance everywhere we went? That is a world we aspire to create—a world where we celebrate the human experience in all its exquisite variety.

Those of us who speak many languages know that to speak someone else's mother tongue fluently is to gain access into a culture in a deep and intimate way. We see it in the faces of people surprised when we reveal fluency in their language. Their eyes, minds, and hearts open to you in a way that says, "You see me. You value the language of my people. You are more than I expected." When you have linguistic fluency, you share a cultural perspective and access to ideas that cannot be translated into other languages. Concepts are literally lost in translation.

We hope that we have given you access to a new language, both in the terminology of subtle acts of exclusion and in the interpersonal tools you can use to make deeper, more authentic connections with the people around you. Remember, the goal is less about avoiding ever committing an SAE and more about being receptive to feedback and willing to disrupt the social and professional equilibrium by speaking up when you witness them. Only once we have large-scale SAE accountability will we be closer to a more equitable and inclusive world.

You were bold enough to finish this book and hopefully experience a mind shift, no matter how subtle. Now we invite you to take the next brave step and act on the lessons you've learned. Because if you embrace the lessons and hold on to the vision we have shared, you may also experience a heart shift. We know that is scary to some people, but it doesn't have to be. A heart shift may well be what more of us need to genuinely embrace each other as one human family. You will know it has happened when you begin to see beauty in places where you once saw fear—friend where you once saw foe— and family in every place you go.

NOTES

1 Pierce, C. M. (1974). Psychiatric problems of the Black minority. In S. Arieti (Ed.), *American handbook of psychiatry* (pp. 512–523). New York, NY: Basic Books.

2 A "trigger warning" is a heads-up that is given (usually to students) about material they are going to see, read, or discuss, that might trigger strong negative or upsetting reactions. It allows people to prepare themselves emotionally or to even remove themselves from the situation. For example, if students are assigned a book that describes a sexual assault, a professor may give a trigger warning, and if someone has experienced trauma from a sexual assault themselves, this might help them better emotionally navigate the assignment. Trigger warnings are not directly linked to microaggressions, but are often lumped together with them by critics.

3 Chait, J. (2015, January 26). Not a very p.c. thing to say: How the language police are perverting liberalism. *New York Magazine*. Retrieved from *http://www.nymag.com*

4 Cooley, L. (2018, June 11). Justice Department attacks microaggression culture in campus free speech lawsuit. *The Washington Examiner*. Retrieved from *http://www.washingtonexaminer.com*

5 Lukianoff, G., & Haidt, J. (2019). *The Coddling of the American Mind*. New York, NY: Penguin Books.

6 Wang, J., Leu, J., & Shoda, Y. (2011). When the seemingly innocuous "stings": Racial microaggressions and their emotional consequences. *Personality and Social Psychology Bulletin, 37*(12), 1666–1678.

7 Lilienfeld, S. O. (2017). Microaggressions: Strong claims, inadequate evidence. *Perspectives on Psychological Science, 12*(1), 138–169.

8 Hunt, V., Prince, S., Dixon-Fyle, S., & Yee, L. (2018, January). *Delivering through diversity*. McKinsey & Company. Retrieved from *http://www.mckinsey.com*

9 See Banaji, M. R., & Greenwald, A. G. (2016). *Blindspot: Hidden biases of good people*. New York, NY: Bantam, and Kahneman, D. (2011). *Thinking, fast and slow*. New York, NY: Farrar, Straus and Giroux.

10 Ross, H. J. (2014). *Everyday bias: Identifying and navigating unconscious judgments in our daily lives*. Lanham, MD: Rowman & Littlefield.

CHAPTER 2

1 Ruiz, D. M. (1997). *The four agreements: A practical guide to personal freedom* (a Toltec wisdom book). San Rafael, CA: Amber-Allen Publishing.

CHAPTER 3

1 Aguilar, L. C. (2006). *Ouch! That stereotype hurts: Communicating respectfully in a diverse world*. Dallas, TX: The Walk The Talk Company.

2 The national organization Showing Up for Racial Justice also uses this language of "calling in" rather than "calling out" to get more white people involved and invested in racial justice.

3 See, for example, Ross, L. (2019, August 17). I'm a Black feminist. I think call-out culture is toxic. [Opinion]. *New York Times*. Retrieved from *http://www.nytimes.com*

CHAPTER 4

1 Edmondson, A. (1999). Psychological safety and learning behavior in work teams. *Administrative Science Quarterly, 44*(2), 350–383.

CHAPTER 5

1 Fausto-Sterling, A. (2000). *Sexing the body: Gender politics and the construction of sexuality*. New York, NY: Basic Books.

2 Brain Architecture. (n.d.). Retrieved from *http://developingchild.harvard.edu/science/key-concepts/brain-architecture/*

3 Lockman, D. (2019, May 4). What "good" dads get away with. [Opinion]. *New York Times*. Retrieved from *http://www.nytimes.com*

4 Chira, S. (2017, June 14). The universal phenomenon of men interrupting women. *New York Times*. Retrieved from *http://www.nytimes.com*

5 David, E. J. R. (Ed.). (2014). *Internalized oppression: The psychology of marginalized groups*. New York, NY: Springer.

6 Dorn, A. (2018, January 16). Girl, no you don't. Retrieved from *http://www.medium.com/@dorn.anna/girl-no-you-dont-2e21e826c62c*

7   Centers for Disease Control and Prevention. (2016). Sexual identity, sex of sexual contacts, and health-risk behaviors among students in grades 9–12: Youth risk behavior surveillance. Atlanta, GA: US Department of Health and Human Services.

8   SXSW. (2019, March 9). *The future is fluid: How gender and sexuality has changed* [Audio file]. Retrieved from *http://schedule.sxsw.com/2019/events /PP92683*

9   Brannen, S. S. (2008). *Uncle Bobby's wedding.* New York, NY: G.P. Putnam's Sons.

CHAPTER 6

1   Gould, S. J. (1996). *The mismeasure of man* (Rev. and expanded). New York, NY: W.W. Norton & Company.

2   Wilson, J. P., Hugenberg, K., & Rule, N. O. (2017). Racial bias in judgments of physical size and formidability: From size to threat. *Journal of Personality and Social Psychology, 113*(1), 59.

3   Cheryan, S., & Monin, B. (2005). Where are you really from?: Asian Americans and identity denial. *Journal of Personality and Social Psychology, 89*(5), 717–730.

CHAPTER 7

1   Swinbourne, C. (2015, February 5). Disabled people aren't here to inspire you. [Opinion]. *The Guardian.*

2   Take the pledge. (2019). Retrieved from *http://www.stopmakingitweird.com /take-the-pledge*

CHAPTER 9

1   Fry, R. (2018, April 11). Millennials are the largest generation in the U.S. labor force. Retrieved from *http://www.pewresearch.org/fact-tank/2018/04 /11/millennials-largest-generation-us-labor-force/*

2   We wanted to point out the term "blind spot," which may be considered an example of a subtle act of exclusion around disability that people often do not even notice. In fact, the authors themselves had used the term several times in the writing of this book without thinking and edited it out during revisions.

3   Wisdom 2.0. (2018, July 2). *Wisdom @ work: The modern elder* [Video file]. Retrieved from *http://www.youtube.com/watch?v=PD97_QGQXFM*

4   Honeyman, R. (2019, April 18). White people: Let's talk about white supremacy. Retrieved from *http://www.medium.com/@RyanHoneyman /white-people-lets-talk-about-white-supremacy-b4088a2630f3*

GLOSSARY

ally: In the context of SAE, someone who speaks up about SAE when they themselves are not the subject.

attributional ambiguity: The sense of anxiety created when someone with a marginalized identity is unable to discern whether something happened because of said identity or some other random factors.

bias: Favor toward or prejudice against one thing, person, or group.

bystander: In the context of SAE, an observer who chooses not to speak up.

cisgender: When a person's gender identity aligns with their biological sex.

cultural fluency: Understanding of cultural context that allows one to communicate cross-culturally or with those who are different from oneself.

culture: Ideas among a group of people of what everything is and how it works.

DEI: Diversity, equity, and inclusion.

diversity: All the ways that people are both the same or different.

emotional intelligence: The ability to identify, use, understand, and manage emotions in positive ways.

emotional labor: Managing or stifling your own (or others') emotions to maintain a healthy environment.

equity: Everyone gets what they need to be successful.

ethnicity: A social construct about where people think their ancestors came from that forms their ideas about heritage/culture.

explicit acts of exclusion: Things that people do purposely to exclude, including acts that can be objectively labeled as racist, or hate crimes, or intimidation.

gender: A social construct about how people identify and present, based on conceptions of biological sex; does not have to correlate to sex.

gender nonbinary: People who experience their gender identity and/or gender expression as falling outside the binary categories of man and woman. They may define their gender as falling somewhere in between man and woman, or they may define it as wholly different from these terms.

inclusion: When people feel valued, respected, and part of a group.

individual contributor: Working as an individual, without line-management responsibilities, but still benefiting the organization as a whole.

intentional acts of inclusion: Consciously making the effort to act in a way that promotes inclusion.

internalized marginalization: Hearing a negative stereotype about your own identity so often that you adopt or affirm that stereotype.

intersectionality: The overlapping systems of discrimination and bias present for a person of multiple marginalized identities.

marginalized identities: The parts of who you are that are either legally protected by, for instance, Title VII laws in the United States (race, sex, religion, age, etc.), or any identity dimension that causes large parts of society to treat you as "less than," or like a second class citizen, unequal to others.

microaggressions: A term used for brief verbal or behavioral indignities, whether intentional or unintentional, that express implicit derogatory or negative ideas and insults toward people with marginalized identities.

oppression: Exerting power over others in an unjust way to maintain your own status.

privilege: Any advantage that an individual or group has that eases (or does not hinder) their success, advancement, or path in life.

psychological safety: A shared belief held by members of a team that the team is safe for interpersonal risk taking.

race: A social construct about groups of people that are assumed to have common biology.

SAE accountability system: Speaking up in a way that holds people accountable with productive, open, and civil conversations based on established best practice guidelines.

SAE initiator: The person who says or who nonverbally does the SAE.

SAE observer: Anyone who overhears or sees the SAE.

SAE subject: The person or group that is excluded by the SAE.

sex: Biological differences around genitalia.

sexuality: Who people are attracted to sexually and romantically.

social construct: An idea that is not based on objective reality but that people think does reflect reality because it becomes part of the cultural common sense of what is real and how things work.

stereotyped expectation: The assumption and expectation that people will behave according to the stereotype or trope associated with their identities.

structural exclusion: Inequality that is perpetuated because it is written into laws and policies.

subtle acts of exclusion (SAE): A new term for "microaggressions": The subtle things that people say and do, perhaps unintentionally, that have the effect of excluding others based on their marginalized dimensions of identity.

taxonomy: Framework or guide.

trigger warning: A heads-up that is given (usually to students) about material they are going to see, read, or discuss that might trigger strong negative or upsetting reactions. It allows people to prepare themselves emotionally or to even remove themselves from the situation.

unconscious bias: An unknown, automatic preference for, or against, a person, a group of people, or an entire demographic group. Though unaware you have it, unconscious (or implicit) bias can influence the way you think and behave.

victim culture: The idea that people are too sensitive and claim victimhood whenever possible.

ACKNOWLEDGMENTS

TIFFANY JANA

First, I must thank God for inspiring me to add this fourth book to my body of work. I thank Michael Baran for agreeing to go on this journey with me. Coauthorship is no small endeavor, and I appreciate him for his grace and patience while we made it happen. Thank you to Jillian Abel for diving in as a research assistant and keeping things moving during the launch and tours for my two previous books. To the indomitable TMI Portfolio team for bearing with me through my authorship journey. I want to acknowledge my family for always believing in my capacity to express myself creatively, and my friends, at whose expense my books tend to be written. When I am writing books I tend to miss the parties, gatherings, and events that strengthen bonds. So thank you for allowing me to put this work into the world and giving up some of our time together. And to all of the people forced to endure the onslaught of SAE as we walk through daily life, I pray that this book offers a small light in the darkness.

MICHAEL BARAN

I thank my wife, Jill, who provided the time, the loving support, the sunshine, and the intense conversations for these ideas to grow and find their way into this book. I thank my children, Rio, Solomon, Raphael, and Carmelo, for keeping me balanced and laughing and hopeful for the future in the way that they recognize and fight against the subtle exclusions they see in their orbits. I thank Tiffany Jana for partnering with me on this undertaking. The way

Tiffany does this work with unrelenting ferocity for the mission and a generosity of spirit is a model for us all to follow. This book would not be a book, in all the meanings you can imagine, without Steve Piersanti and the Berrett-Koehler team, and I am so appreciative. My inQUEST colleagues, especially longtime friend and collaborator Michael Handelman, push, challenge, and support me (and one another) in the best possible ways, and I am proud to call them my work family. I can't imagine what it would have been like to study the subtleties of culture without Bradd Shore or the intricacies of cognition and race without Lawrence Hirschfeld. I thank so many of you (Aimee Cox, I'm looking at you) who pushed me to use my privilege and my research to try and make the world a better place. Special acknowledgment to those who have shared their stories of subtle and not-so-subtle exclusion with me over the years. Your sharing has led to this book, which I hope is a valuable tool as we move toward a more equitable future together.

INDEX

ABOUT THE AUTHORS

TIFFANY AND MICHAEL hit it off right away when they met for the first time in 2015. Michael had developed a gamified learning tool around race and ethnicity, and Tiffany was interested in learning more. Michael said goodbye to his family and chickens for the day and drove down from his small iris flower farm in Maryland to Tiffany's office in Richmond, Virginia. They had a deep connection around the passion for DEI work; the drive to do the work differently and better, using the best platforms; and the need for a strong evidence base to understand how things really work and the best practices to make them better. Tiffany included Michael's race education program in their first book, *Overcoming Bias*, in 2016. They kept in touch and presented together in a panel on pushing the boundaries of tech in D&I work at the Forum on Workplace Inclusion in 2018. It was at that conference, talking about Tiffany's second and third books, that they began to explicitly talk about the idea of writing a book together.

The idea for rethinking the concept of microaggressions came during their first conversations with Steve Piersanti at Berrett-Koehler Publishers. Both Tiffany and Michael had independently held deep frustrations with the term and the way it was being used in popular culture and in D&I work. Michael even had a running document of possible alternatives. He sent that to Tiffany, who put their own spin on it, and the concept of SAE started to take shape.

This book brings together the different personal experiences and professional backgrounds of Tiffany and Michael. Tiffany identifies with multiple marginalized identities and walks through the world experiencing SAE around those identities on a daily basis. They bring that sensibility and depth of understanding to the way they approach these issues. Michael, on the other hand, walks through life with privilege in that regard, perceived as the straight white cisgender man that he is. As such, he researches and listens attentively to the stories that others tell him about their experiences. And he notices the way that people with normative identities are unguarded around him, allowing him to deeply understand bias and to meet people where they are to communicate effectively to them and maybe even change the way they think.

The book also benefits from the range of professional experiences that Tiffany and Michael cover. Tiffany, a doctor of management in organizational leadership, founded TMI Consulting, Inc., in 2003 and has more recently founded TMI Portfolio and Loom Technologies, Inc., specializing in diversity and inclusion, leadership, using metrics to gauge organizational equity, and unconscious bias. Michael got his doctorate in cultural anthropology with a certificate in cognitive psychology, researching how culture and cognition interact in the way that people learn about categories of difference and bias, and how to most effectively communicate to change patterns of thinking. He spent some time in academia, teaching at Harvard University and the University of Michigan. He also spent several years doing applied cultural research for the FrameWorks

Institute and the American Institutes for Research. While working at these institutions, he also started consulting for organizations around diversity and inclusion issues and now does that work full time as a senior partner and digital solutions lead at inQUEST Consulting. Both authors and their respective companies are constantly pushing themselves to do this DEI work with innovative ideas, state of the art technologies and platforms, and a true spirit of collaboration that they hope comes through in this book.

ABOUT THE TMI PORTFOLIO OF COMPANIES

TMI CONSULTING, INC., is a 100 percent minority owned company, founded in 2003, and has been certified as the world's first diversity focused B Corporation since 2012. TMI Consulting has earned national and international recognition for its efficacy and innovation. The company pioneered the use of innovative technology and development of proprietary diversity ROI metrics for organizational accountability in diversity, equity, and inclusion. TMI Consulting has expanded its global brand presence under the TMI Portfolio of companies. TMI Portfolio consists of socially responsible, interconnected organizations working to advance cultural inclusivity.

Loom Technologies, a TMI Portfolio company, launched the first full-service DEI software product in 2018 after six years of research and development. The technology company emerged to meet the needs of TMI Consulting's largest, and most geographically dispersed, clients. Loom The Culture Map® helps measure, map, and improve organizational culture using machine learning. The full product includes a DEI Policy Audit and a customizable range of eighty DEI metrics measured across eleven categories. Loom's proprietary roadmap offers clients step-by-step DEI strategy implementation guidance based on the results of each DEI assessment. Clients can implement their inclusion strategy independently or with TMI Consulting's support. The TMI Portfolio of companies leverages strategic partnerships to offer a full slate of supplementary trainings, including selected train-the-trainer curricula and unconscious bias, microaggressions (SAE), digital, and microlearning options.

TMI Consulting offers custom trainings based on all four of Dr. Jana's published books: *Overcoming Bias, Erasing Institutional Bias,* the second edition of *The B Corp Handbook*, and *Subtle Acts of Exclusion*. The TMI Portfolio of companies are also DEI service providers for Gallagher, the global HR consulting firm, and Blue Ocean Brain's microlearning platform. We work reciprocally with these and many other companies to meet the myriad needs of our clients. We don't try to be the best at everything, just diversity, equity, and inclusion. Our strategic allies specialize in the areas adjacent to diversity to offer our clients seamless assistance to meet their unique needs.

As a certified B Corporation, we have an ethical and legal commitment to providing a benefit to society. We measure our triple bottom line (profit, people, and planet) global impact using B Lab's B Impact Assessment. We've been named Best for the World in 2016, 2018, and 2019 for our social and environmental performance.

ABOUT inQUEST CONSULTING

FOUNDED IN 2011, inQUEST Consulting seeks to drive new and innovative thinking in the diversity and inclusion space by bringing together a collective of thought leaders with decades of varied experience working with clients in complex, dynamic environments. Our leadership team comprises nationally recognized thought leaders and master facilitators, certified coaches, and seasoned D&I executives, with backgrounds that range from finance and banking to law, human resources, social sciences, and education technology.

inQUEST is a global D&I firm, supporting clients across a wide range of industries and sizes—startups, large multinational companies, nonprofits, educational institutions, and government agencies. We help individuals, teams, and organizations think, lead, and interact inclusively.

Our range of products and services falls into three main areas:

- **Strategy & Structure:** D&I strategy that's focused on business results (D&I strategy & planning, BRGs, ERG support & design, cultural assessments, ideation & visioning)

- **Education & Experiences:** Energizing experiences that drive culture change (D&I training & design, leadership development, coaching & effectiveness, conferences & events, keynotes, digital learning paths, Contineo gamified training)

- **Bridges & Breakthroughs:** When coming together is difficult but critical (conflict resolution, post-merger alignment, meeting facilitation, sensitive & complex conversations)

We operate on four guiding principles. First, we take a collaborative approach. We partner with leaders and leverage their insights to collaboratively develop creative and practical solutions that work. Second, we tailor solutions to our individual client needs. We know that each organization is different—whether best-in-class for D&I or just getting started. Our services are grounded in common and proven principles, tailored for each organization's unique objectives, culture, and industry. Third, we make trainings people focused and highly engaging. Whether it's our interactive workshops (Unconscious Bias, Conscious Inclusion, Speak Up Culture, etc.), our award-winning gamified training Contineo, or our digital learning paths, our products and services connect and delight employees and thereby increase effectiveness. Finally, we focus on business impact. Bringing diverse perspectives together with genuine inclusion is not only good for individuals but also drives innovation and performance for our client organizations.

Find out more at *www.inquestconsulting.com.*

More from Tiffany Jana

Overcoming Bias

Building Authentic Relationships across Differences

Tiffany Jana and Matthew Freeman

Control, conquer, and prevail!

Everybody's biased. The truth is, we all harbor unconscious assumptions that can get in the way of our good intentions and keep us from building authentic relationships with people different from ourselves. Tiffany Jana and Matthew Freeman use vivid stories and fun (yes, fun!) exercises and activities to help us reflect on our personal experiences and uncover how our hidden biases are formed. By becoming more self-aware, we can control knee-jerk reactions, conquer fears of the unknown, and prevail over closed-mindedness. In the end, Jana and Freeman's central message is that you are *not* the problem—but you can be the solution.

Paperback, ISBN 978-1-62656-725-2
PDF ebook, ISBN 978-1-62656-726-9
Epub ebook, ISBN 978-1-62656-727-6
Digital audio, ISBN 978-1-62656-729-0

BK® Berrett–Koehler Publishers, Inc.
www.bkconnection.com

800.929.2929

Erasing Institutional Bias
How to Create Systemic Change for Organizational Inclusion
Tiffany Jana and Ashley Diaz Mejias

Inclusion through action!

All humans have biases, and as a result, so do the institutions we build. Internationally sought-after diversity consultant Tiffany Jana empowers readers to work against institutional bias no matter what their position is in an organization. Building on *Overcoming Bias*, which addressed individual and interpersonal bias, *Erasing Institutional Bias* scales up to foster change in organizations. Jana and coauthor Ashley Diaz Mejias bring together in-depth research on how biases become embedded into the workplace with practical and engaging tools that mobilize readers toward action. They confront persistent systemic biases—such as racism, sexism, hiring and advancement bias, and cultures of aggression—and offer solutions for controlling them. In a world divided, this book is designed to raise awareness about inequality and hold ourselves accountable for creating a world that works for everyone.

Paperback, ISBN 978-1-5230-9757-9
PDF ebook, ISBN 978-1-5230-9758-6
ePub ebook, ISBN 978-1-5230-9759-3
Digital audio, ISBN 978-1-5230-9761-6

BK Berrett–Koehler Publishers, Inc.
www.bkconnection.com

800.929.29

Dear reader,

Thank you for picking up this book and welcome to the worldwide BK community! You're joining a special group of people who have come together to create positive change in their lives, organizations, and communities.

What's BK all about?

Our mission is to connect people and ideas to create a world that works for all.

Why? Our communities, organizations, and lives get bogged down by old paradigms of self-interest, exclusion, hierarchy, and privilege. But we believe that can change. That's why we seek the leading experts on these challenges—and share their actionable ideas with you.

A welcome gift

To help you get started, we'd like to offer you a **free copy** of one of our bestselling ebooks:

www.bkconnection.com/welcome

When you claim your **free ebook**, you'll also be subscribed to our blog.

Our freshest insights

Access the best new tools and ideas for leaders at all levels on our blog at ideas.bkconnection.com.

Sincerely,

Your friends at Berrett-Koehler